50 Ways to Improve Student Behavior

Simple Solutions to Complex Challenges

Annette Breaux and Todd Whitaker

EYE ON EDUCATION
6 DEPOT WAY WEST, SUITE 106
LARCHMONT, NY 10538
(914) 833–0551
(914) 833–0761 fax
www.eyeoneducation.com

Library of Congress Cataloging-in-Publication Data

Breaux, Annette L.
  50 ways to improve student behavior : simple solutions to complex challenges / Annette Breaux and Todd Whitaker.
      p. cm.
  Includes bibliographical references.
  ISBN 978-1-59667-132-4
  1. Effective teaching—United States—Case studies. 2. Interaction analysis in education I. Whitaker, Todd, 1959– II. Title. III. Title: Fifty ways to improve student behavior.
  LB1025.3.B74 2009
  371.39'3—dc22

                                                        2009030115

10 9 8 7 6 5 4 3 2 1

All poetry in this book is the original work of Annette Breaux.

Also Available from EYE ON EDUCATION

What Great Teachers Do *Differently*:
14 Things That Matter Most
Todd Whitaker

Seven Simple Secrets: What the Best Teachers Know and Do!
Annette L. Breaux and Todd Whitaker

What Great Principals Do *Differently*:
15 Things That Matter Most
Todd Whitaker

101 Answers for New Teachers and Their Mentors:
Effective Teaching Tips for Daily Classroom Use
Annette L. Breaux

Dealing with Difficult Teachers, Second Edition
Todd Whitaker

Great Quotes for Great Educators
Todd Whitaker

Dealing with Difficult Parents
Todd Whitaker

Teaching Matters: Motivating and Inspiring Yourself
Todd and Beth Whitaker

REAL Teachers, REAL Challenges, REAL Solutions: 25 Ways
to Handle the Challenges of the Classroom Effectively
Annette and Elizabeth Breaux

The Poetry of Annette Breaux
Annette L. Breaux

The Four Core Factors for School Success
Todd Whitaker and Jeffrey Zoul

Meet the Authors

Annette Breaux is one of the most entertaining and informative authors and speakers in education today. She leaves her audiences with practical techniques to implement in their classrooms immediately. Administrators agree that they see results from teachers the next day.

A former classroom teacher, curriculum coordinator, and author of Louisiana FIRST, a statewide induction program for new teachers, Annette now serves as the teacher induction coordinator for Nicholls State University in Thibodaux, Louisiana. Annette has coauthored a book with Dr. Harry Wong on new teacher induction.

Her other writings include *101 Answers for New Teachers and Their Mentors*; *REAL Teachers, REAL Challenges, REAL Solutions*; *The Poetry of Annette Breaux: Tips and Poems for Teachers and Students*; *10 Days to Maximum Teaching Success*; and *Seven Simple Secrets: What the BEST Teachers Know and Do!*

Teachers who have read Annette's writings or heard Annette speak agree that they come away with user-friendly information, heartfelt inspiration, and a much-needed reminder that theirs is the most noble of all professions—teaching.

Dr. Todd Whitaker is recognized as a leading presenter in education. His message about the importance of teaching has resonated with hundreds of thousands of educators around the world. Todd is a professor of educational leadership at Indiana State University in Terre Haute, Indiana. He has spent his life pursuing his love of education by studying effective teachers and principals.

Prior to coming to Indiana, he taught and coached at the middle and high school levels in Missouri. Following his teaching experience, he served as a middle school and high school principal. He also served as a middle school coordinator.

One of the nation's leading authorities on staff motivation, teacher leadership, and principal effectiveness, Todd has written eighteen educational books including the national best seller, *What Great Teachers Do Differently*. Other titles include *Dealing With Difficult Teachers*; *Teaching Matters*; *Great Quotes for Great Educators*; *What Great Principals Do Differently*; *Motivating & Inspiring Teachers*; and *Dealing With Difficult Parents*.

Todd is married to Beth, also a former teacher and principal, who is a professor of Elementary Education at Indiana State University. They are the parents of Katherine, Madeline, and Harrison.

"Life could be so wonderful if my students would just behave
But at the rate they're going right now, I'll see an early grave
They talk, they laugh, they hit, they throw
What will I do? I do not know
I beg, I plead, I punish, I scream
Oh help me, please, I'm losing steam

What? You have the answers to get students to behave?
Some simple things that I can do? My sanity you'll save?"

Yes, we think that we can help to ease your needless pain
We write this book with you in mind. Allow us to explain
That if you take our words to heart and do what we suggest
We think you'll soon be witnessing behavior at its best!

Annette Breaux and Todd Whitaker

What This Book Will Do for You

Want to be a better teacher who has better student behavior and better student learning? Want less stress in your life? Want an overall happy, more effectively and efficiently run classroom? Want better student motivation? Then this book is for you.

This book focuses on you, the teacher. It is written for teachers who teach students of all grade levels, genders, ethnic backgrounds, and social upbringings. It is not designed to make you the perfect teacher. There is no such person. It is not designed to help you mold the perfect students. There are no such people. Rather, it is designed to provide you with the tools to improve, not perfect, student behavior in your classroom. As an added benefit, **when behavior improves, so does learning**. So we intend to help you to improve both student behavior and learning. We also believe you'll soon realize that by applying our suggestions your teaching will improve dramatically.

We sincerely believe that it is your goal, as one who wants to touch lives and make a difference, to be as effective as you can be. We believe that you, as one called *teacher*, possess the ability and the desire to be the teacher every student remembers.

So if you want to be a better teacher with better student behavior and, as an added bonus, improved student learning, read on!

Contents

Preface

"If only the parents cared more! If only the principal would *do* something about the misbehavior of students! If only the teacher who has my students before me wouldn't get them so riled up that they're wild when they get to me!" Sound familiar? We hear these opinions often and maybe even state them often ourselves. But the bottom line is that **we really can't *do* anything about them**. Whether we think that some parents lack good parenting skills, or that our principal should do more, or that our coworkers should be more competent, we really have no control over such situations.

The focus of this book is on simple strategies you can use to become better at the one thing you absolutely do have control over—what goes on every day within the four walls of your classroom. Regardless of outside forces, regardless of home lives, regardless of what is or is not going on in the front office, it is the teacher who controls what goes on every day in the classroom.

But why don't students just behave? Well, the fact remains that we teach children, and children do child-like things. They don't make adult-like decisions; they don't do what's necessarily right or best for them; they do like to push our buttons; and they are not, for the most part, self-motivated or self-disciplined. That's why they need us!

A speaker was addressing a group of teachers, and one teacher raised her hand and said, "Well, all of these things you are saying are fine, well, and good. And maybe your suggestions would work with some students, but you don't understand. I have *no* parental support, and it's impossible to teach these students when their parents aren't backing me." The speaker asked a simple question: "So you're saying that if an orphanage opened next door to this school tomorrow, you could not teach those children?" A hush fell over the audience and over that teacher. Of course those students would still be teachable. Might they have issues to deal with that are unlike those of children who are reared by their parents? They might. But they're still reachable and teachable. Just as you have to actually reach the summit of the mountain before you can stand on it, and just as you have to reach your vacation's destination before you can do your sightseeing, **you have to reach a student before you can teach him**. Each student brings his own set of issues, his own dreams, his own strengths, his own shortcomings, his own abilities, and his own lack of abilities. But we believe that *each* child is someone special. Each child deserves a chance, and then a second one, and a third, and a fourth. ***Each* child deserves a teacher who believes in him.** If you are reading this book, we believe you are that teacher.

1

Meet and Greet

A Point to Ponder

"When I retire, I want to be a Wal-Mart greeter." We know you've heard it before. You may have even said it! But have you ever really analyzed why so many teachers continue to say this? We have.

Stores like Wal-Mart actually hire people to pretend to be happy to see you, a stranger, as you enter the store. In fact, these people possess the jobs that many teachers say they want to have when they retire. The reason so many teachers say they want to retire and be a Wal-Mart greeter is twofold: (1) The Wal-Mart greeter looks happy. (2) The Wal-Mart greeter looks stress-free! Who wouldn't want a job where he felt happy and stress-free?

Now consider *why* Wal-Mart pays people to greet its customers. Wal-Mart does this because of the simple fact that **happy customers who feel wanted and welcome are more likely to buy what is being sold and will happily return to buy even more**. Period. This is why you are greeted when you walk into a restaurant, when you step onto an airplane, and when you enter any other establishment that puts concerted thought into making its customers feel happy and welcome.

So wouldn't this same concept work with students? And shouldn't we be putting concerted thought into making our students (customers) feel happy and welcome every time they enter our classrooms? Don't we want them to want to "buy" what we are "selling"? Don't we want them to **want** to come back? The answers to those questions are *yes, yes, yes,* and *yes*!

Classroom Solution/Strategy

!

So let's bring this simple strategy into the classroom. In our observations of teachers, we have found that most teachers claim that they greet their students every day. The fact is that some do, and others don't. So let's first establish what greeting does *not* mean. Some teachers stand at their classroom doors and, as the students arrive, say things like, "Let's go. Your work is on the board. Get busy as soon as you get into the room. Hurry. Let's get moving. The bell is about to ring." This, our fellow teachers, is *not* greeting. Rather, it is the equivalent of saying, "Welcome to my torture chamber!" Any student who is rushed into the classroom in this oh-so-unwelcoming manner will hardly feel like you want him in your classroom! Students not feeling wanted? That is a recipe for misbehavior, and class has not even begun! But the foundation has been laid and the little rascals are scheming.

Now, let's look at what greeting *does* mean. The very best teachers, the ones who always seem to have the fewest behavior problems, know the simple strategy that stores such as Wal-Mart know: If the teacher (greeter) looks happy to see his or her students (customers) every day and can actually make the students feel wanted and valued in the classroom, then the students are much more likely to "buy" what the teacher is "selling" and are more apt to want to return to that particular class the next day and the day after!

So here's a simple way to greet your students every day. Don't reinvent the wheel. Just do what the most successful teachers do. Simply stand at your classroom door, every day, every class period, and say things like, "Hello. How are you? Thank you for coming to class. Nice outfit. I love your new haircut. Jason, I'm so happy you're back today. I missed you yesterday!" Okay, so you prayed last night that Jason would *never* come back, but the important thing is that Jason does not know that! He believes that you are happy to see him, and therefore he will be more likely to behave.

The truth is that students are less likely to misbehave in a classroom where they feel wanted and valued. To think that the simple act of "greeting" someone can solve so many problems! It can. The fact is that **if you consistently greet your students every day, then you will soon decrease your discipline problems drastically**. Anyone who does not believe this fact is not greeting students every day. Now, we do want to warn you that if you tend to be a little negative with your students and do not typically greet them every day with a smile on your face, this new approach will confuse your students at first. It will take more than one day of greeting your students to convince them that you are a "changed" person. But stick with it! The results will be worth it.

Is it possible that your "greeting" may be a little phony? Probably. Are you *really* that happy to see every student every day? Possibly not. But remember, we were hired to be actors and actresses! Oh, and just so you know, the Wal-Mart greeter is probably not overly happy to see you either! The flight attendant is possibly tired and hoping for a fairly empty flight. But here you are, yet another passenger! However, *you* should never know that that greeting was possibly a little overexuberant. You deserve to feel welcome and wanted and valued. Make your students feel the same way—every day! Even if you're faking it just a little, you will soon find that the more you "fake it," the more you will actually begin to feel happier, and thus your greetings will become more genuine. What a bonus!

Oh, and what more does it cost to tell them good-bye as they leave your room each day? If they arrive and leave on a happy note, better behavior you will promote!

Bottom Line

 If you *want* your students to *want* to be in your classroom, then you have to convince them that you actually want *them* there. You never know when a simple hello will make someone's day more okay!

A Simple "Hi"

Each day when I entered her classroom, she smiled and said hello
Just what that gesture meant to me, she truly could not know
She did not know that she and only she made me feel wanted
That *her* smile got me through a time in life when I felt daunted
That life at home was way too tough for any kid to take
That her classroom was my refuge, that my happiness was fake
That for her I put my best foot forward, even when times were rough
That my smile was a façade to hide my pain, for I was tough
But even though she never knew, it meant so much to me
That there was one place in my life where someone wanted me
Wanted me to be there, wanted me to learn
Wanted to help me realize there were good things I could earn
For beyond the books and content, I learned that year that I
Was someone who, to someone, was worth a simple "Hi."

2

A Letter of Introduction

A Point to Ponder

Imagine being the parent of a school-age child and receiving a letter in the mail over the summer months from your child's prospective teacher saying who she is, what she wants for your child, what she believes about teaching, and just how happy she is to be teaching your precious angel.

Imagine being a child and receiving a letter from your prospective teacher saying how happy she is that you will be in her class and how anxious she is to meet you, to get to know you, and to teach you.

Think back to how many letters like this you actually received, as a parent or a student. Not too many, if any, right? Well, here are a few things to consider:

- ◆ Parents want to believe that their children are in the hands of competent, caring, trustworthy teachers.

- ◆ Children want to believe that their teachers are people who are excited to teach them and happy to have them in class.

- ◆ Parents who believe that you care about their children are much more likely to work cooperatively with you.

- ◆ Children who are in the classrooms of teachers they perceive as caring are more likely to exhibit better behavior than children who do not believe that their teachers care about them.

This is not rocket science. Rather, it is human nature. So let's take what we know about human nature and use it in our classrooms to foster better student behavior.

Classroom Solution/Strategy

A simple strategy for setting the stage for good student behavior is to write notes to students and parents before the first day of school. As soon as you receive your class rosters, write two simple notes—one to parents and one to students. Here are two samples:

Dear _____:

My name is Mr./Ms. _____ and I just wanted to say that I am so happy to have the opportunity to be teaching your child in this upcoming school year. I am excited about the school year as we will be…. *(Tell about some of the things you will be accomplishing in your specific subject area.)*

I am honored to be able to teach your child, and I promise to do my best to help him/her become successful and reach his/her full potential. If, at any time, I can be of help to you or answer any questions you may have, please feel free to contact me at _____ *(school's phone number).*

Thank you for allowing me the opportunity to teach your child.

Sincerely,

_____

Dear _____:

My name is Mr./Ms. _____ and I will be your teacher for this upcoming school year. I am so excited that you will be in my class, and I look forward to getting to know you. Please know that I will do my very best to make this school year your best and most successful one ever.

Thank you for being a part of my class. Let's make it a great school year!

Sincerely,

_____

Bottom Line

By taking the time to send such letters, you have just laid the groundwork for a positive start to your school year and a positive relationship with the parents of your students. You may consider asking your principal if the school can pay for the postage. If not, you may consider putting both letters in one envelope. If this is still too much of a financial burden, hand these letters to your students on the very first day of school. **A simple letter can make behavior better—at any age level!**

3

Tools for Rules and Procedures

A Point to Ponder

 Contrary to conventional wisdom, the main problem in the classroom is *not* the lack of obedience on the part of students. Rather, it is the lack of clearly established and consistently enforced rules and procedures on the part of teachers. This is not to say, however, that teachers with clearly established rules and procedures have no discipline challenges. They do. It is to say, however, that teachers with rules and procedures have *far* fewer discipline challenges than their counterparts who lack a clear system of rules and procedures. In fact, the very best teachers, although they do have discipline **challenges**, rarely have discipline **problems**. That's because they know how to avoid letting the challenges ever **become** problems. Their secret? Clear and consistent rules and procedures!

We continue to find that many teachers do not know the difference between a rule and a procedure. Allow us to both clarify and simplify:

♦ A *rule* regulates a serious offense, and there must be a consequence *every* time it is broken.

♦ A *procedure* is simply a way that you want something to be done—the same way, every time.

♦ When a student breaks a rule, the student is punished.

♦ When a student does not follow a procedure, you simply practice the procedure with the student.

♦ You will never want to have more than five rules.

♦ You should have many procedures.

♦ An example of a rule (remember that a rule is something to regulate a serious offense) is *We agree not to hit anyone.* If the rule is broken, there is a definite consequence, and the students know this in advance.

♦ Examples of procedures are how to walk in line, what to do when you have a question, what to do when you need a pencil sharpened, how to get into and out of groups, etc.

Now the problem occurs when teachers confuse the two. On the "Rules Chart," they put statements such as "I will not talk out of turn." Well, talking is actually not a *serious* offense. An aggravating offense? Yes. A serious offense? No. Therefore, it should fall into the category of "procedure." The procedure may state, "We agree to raise our hands and be recognized before speaking." So what do you do if a student talks out of turn? You simply remind him of the procedure and practice again if necessary. In #19, we will discuss what to do if you have a "chronic" talker who does not respond to your little "reminders."

So here it is, plainly and simply: You practice when they forget a procedure, and you punish if they break a rule. That's it.

Classroom Solution/Strategy

 ### Rules

Decide what you would consider to be serious offenses in your classroom. We gave you one example: "We agree not to hit each other." Notice two things: (1) *Hitting someone is a serious offense.* None of us want students displaying any acts of violence in our classrooms. (2) *The rule is stated in a positive way.* Again, try to limit your rules to no more than five. Now introduce your rules to your students, discuss why they are important, and explain the consequences of not following the rules. And then be consistent in enforcing them. Not mean, but consistent.

Procedures

You will not want to establish all of your procedures at one time. This is far too overwhelming for students. Instead, begin with the most important ones and then add a few at a time. In establishing any procedure, there are six simple steps:

1. State the procedure and discuss its importance.

2. Model the procedure. Show your students exactly what it "looks like."

3. Practice the procedure with your students. (Note that this is not something reserved for elementary-level students. Professional football teams practice procedures every day!)

4. Praise them when they follow it and remind them of the procedure when they "forget."

5. Continue to calmly practice the procedure with students when they forget.

6. Remain consistent with your procedures.

If you're going to try this, we suggest that you implement the most important procedure first. Do you know the most important procedure that any teacher can and must have? The most important procedure you can and must have is a **consistent way of securing your students' attention** every time you need it. It is so essential because if you cannot secure their attention, you cannot teach them. So we ask you, "What's the one thing you do every time you want your students' attention?" Do you have one procedure, such as a signal for requesting your students' attention? Do they know what your procedure is and do they respond to it? Or do you try several things such as putting your finger to your lips, then saying "Shhhh" or "I need your attention," or flicking the lights, or a host of *many* other things that teachers do to no avail? There is no "one" correct way of getting your students' attention. However, there are some things that *never* work. Begging, threatening, and warning are ineffective. Whatever your procedure, it needs to be consistent; it must be practiced with your students time and again, and you must never appear "bent out of shape" while using it. (We know a few teachers who literally bend their bodies and their faces out of shape when they get upset. Not a pretty sight!)

Bottom Line

Contrary to the beliefs of far too many teachers, having a good discipline plan, including clear rules and procedures, is not simply about being *nice* vs. *mean*; but rather it is also about being *consistent* vs. *inconsistent*! You see, if you're **nice and inconsistent**, your students will "like" you, but you will not be able to manage them, and therefore you won't be able to teach them. If you're **mean and inconsistent**, you're doomed! If you're **mean and consistent**, you're a little less doomed but still doomed! But if you are both **nice and consistent**, you'll have excellent classroom management. And the fact is that without good management, you cannot teach.

So get your rules and procedures straight, be consistent and don't negotiate, and good behavior will surely await!

4

Are You All Right?

A Point to Ponder

 "Are you all right?" Those four words say "I care about you." What feels better, for any of us, than to know that someone cares about us? What student wouldn't behave better if he felt that his teacher cared about him? Conversely, what student would be motivated to behave well in the classroom of a teacher who didn't care?

Recipe for Good Behavior

Take a misbehaving student, plus a cup of aggravation
Then add a protruding vein in your neck and a sigh of sheer
    frustration
Then mix it all together, boiling it 'til it bubbles
And within a few seconds it's done, and you have multiplied your
    troubles

And if it does not taste good to you, there is an antidote
A recipe for getting the better behavior you're trying to promote:

Take a misbehaving student, and ask him if he's all right
And convince him that you believe in him and you care with all
    your might
When he sees you're not out to get him, believing that you are
    sincere
You'll be tasting better behavior for the duration of the year!

Classroom Solution/Strategy

!

The "Are You All Right" technique is simple, is effective, and is based on the premise that **students who believe you actually care about them are much more apt to behave better.** Here's what you do: The next time a student is behaving inappropriately in your classroom, take him outside of the classroom and ask, in a very sincere tone, "Are you all right?" (It is vitally important that you appear genuine and concerned.) You may see a surprised look on the student's face. But almost always, the student will answer, "Yes." Then follow this by saying, "Well, the reason I'm asking is that the way you were behaving in class was inappropriate and not at all like you." (Okay, so maybe you're stretching the truth a little, as this particular behavior was very typical of that student, but we think you can see where we're going with this....) "And so I knew that for you to be acting that way, something had to be bothering you. And I just wanted you to know that if you need to talk about what's bothering you, I'm here for you." That's it. Now you simply go back into the classroom.

Have you dealt with the misbehavior? Yes. You made it clear that the behavior was inappropriate. Will the student's behavior improve? Almost always!

Please note that what you did *not* do was also very important. You did not dare him to do it again, you did not act personally offended, you did not threaten him, and you did not belittle him. You expressed nothing but caring and concern about his inappropriate behavior.

A high school teacher shared this story with us.

> I heard you talking about the "Are You All Right" technique, and I honestly did not believe it would work. I teach at-risk students, and their behavior is some of the worst I've ever seen. I had a student return to school after the Christmas holidays, and for three straight days, he did absolutely no work in class. For the most part, he kept his head on his desk and slept. I was getting more angry and frustrated by the minute, so I decided to try the "Are You All Right" technique, believing, of course, that it would not work. I took him out into the hallway and asked, "Are you all right?" The student began to cry and said, "No, I'm not. I have cancer. It was diagnosed over the holidays, and it's a very aggressive type of cancer. They started my chemotherapy, and it's making me really sleepy. But I really want to be here because I don't know how much time I have left." (Tears fell from this teacher's face as he shared his story.) The teacher continued, "I asked him, 'Why didn't you tell me?' And the student answered, 'I didn't know you cared.'"

Now did this teacher care? Of course he did. We later learned that he began taking this student to his chemotherapy treatments whenever possible. But the fact is that just because you care doesn't mean the students automatically know that. Many students come to us assuming that we don't care. So it is our job to convince them that we do.

Bottom Line

The fact that some students assume that their teachers don't care about them often leads to the following:

- Misbehavior
- Indignant attitudes
- Disrespect
- Apathy
- Lack of motivation

The fact that some teachers know how to show their students that they care often leads to the following:

- Good behavior
- Positive attitudes
- Respect
- Interest
- Motivation

Which would you prefer? You decide!

5

Stay Near, Dear

A Point to Ponder

 It has been proven, time and again, that **a physical barrier creates a mental barrier**, every time. Let us explain. It you walk into a room to meet with someone and that person is seated behind a desk, it is more intimidating than if that person gets up from his desk and comes and sits next to you. Once the barrier (the desk) has been removed, the situation becomes less intimidating. If you listen to a speaker who stands behind a podium, it does not "feel" the same as if that speaker actually walks out into the audience and interacts with the participants. Sitting across the table from someone at a meal is not as intimate as sitting next to that person at the table. Get the idea? Then let's bring that into the classroom.

Classroom Solution/Strategy

 Far too often, and usually without realizing it, teachers separate themselves from their students with a physical barrier, be it a desk or a podium. Now, granted, the students are not consciously thinking that you have created a physical (and mental) barrier. Their behavior, however, says that they do recognize it at a subconscious level. **In classrooms where teachers separate themselves physically from their students, behavior suffers.**

Want a simple solution? Get out from behind your desk or podium and get right in the middle of your students and teach away! This simple act, on your part, will send a message that you are "right in there" with them. Also, the closer you are in proximity to a student, the less likely he is to misbehave. Try it. If a student is behaving inappropriately, simply walk over and pause next to him—without giving him "the eye," of course. Simply continue teaching, without breaking stride, but do it standing closer to him. You will almost always see improved behavior. That's because **students find it more difficult to misbehave when an adult is standing right next to them**.

Here's something else to consider: It has also been proven that **teachers get into their own "comfort zones" and tend to gravitate toward one spot in their classrooms**. This is never effective, because it has also been proven that most discipline problems occur farthest away from the teacher. The solution? Stay on the move! You don't need to run around your classroom constantly, but rather move purposefully around the room as you teach.

Here's a question to ask yourself: If someone walked into your room and asked your students, "Where does your teacher usually stand?," would the students be able to answer that question? The answer should be, "She's all over. She never stands in the same place for long." Regrettably, most teachers, if they are honest, will realize that they do tend to gravitate to one spot in the classroom. So get out of your "comfort zone," and make a concerted effort to get closer to your students and to move among them as you teach.

Bottom Line

 The closer you are to your students, the more engaged they will be, the better their behavior will be, and the less tempted they will be to "scheme." It is true that "While the cat's away, the mice will play." Stay near, dear, and remove those physical barriers. Save sitting behind your desk for before and after school hours. The closer you get, the less you'll fret over behavior tribulations and, thus, frustrations.

6

Believe in Them!

A Point to Ponder

- Many students do not believe that their teachers actually believe in them.

- Many students do not believe that their parents actually believe in them.

- Many students do not believe that any adult actually believes in them.

- Many students, therefore, do not believe in themselves.

- Students who do not believe in themselves tend to have more behavior problems.

- Students who *do* believe in themselves actually cause fewer discipline challenges for teachers.

Children do not automatically and innately believe in themselves. They look to their role models, adults in their lives, to determine their sense of "worthiness." **If a student lacks positive role models at home, his only hope may lie in the hands of his teachers.** When students lack positive role models at home, they tend to be more difficult to deal with regarding behavior. Thus, the teacher's job may become more challenging. But no one said that teaching was easy. It's not. Every child, however, deserves to have an adult who believes in him. And even if a child does have positive role models at home and actually does believe in himself, one teacher who does not believe in that child can upset the whole equation! When we consider the fact that school-age children spend so much of their time with their teachers (and often more waking hours with their teachers than with their parents), it is not difficult to understand why teachers have such powerful influence on students' lives. And also, when we consider the fact that you have to *reach* the child before you can *teach* the child, then it should be your main goal, as a teacher, to reach every child you teach. So how do you reach a child? **You reach a child by convincing him that you believe in him.**

Classroom Solution/Strategy

Okay, so we've established the fact that you must convince all students that you believe in them in order to reach them and thus teach them. *All* students! **So what does it look like when a teacher believes in his/her students?**

- ♦ Lots of smiling on the part of the teacher.
- ♦ Lots of encouragement and "You can do it" statements.
- ♦ Lots of support on the part of the teacher.
- ♦ Lots of patience on the part of the teacher.
- ♦ Lots of saying "I believe in you" to students.

Do you want a student to believe in himself? Then actually *tell* him that you believe in him, that you will not give up on him, that you understand his struggles, and that you are there for him.

We continue to find that far too many teachers forget to do this—to tell and show their students that they actually believe in them. It's a simple thing to do. So do it!

Bottom Line

Students who believe in themselves behave better. Teachers who believe in their students have fewer discipline problems. If you are thinking, "It can't be that if I do something as simple as believing in my students that I will see improved behavior," then you have obviously never tried it. So try it, and you will soon become a *believer*!

Believe In Me

I didn't understand, but my teacher just moved on
She said she had no time to wait for the light on me to dawn
So on she moved and there I stayed; she left me in the dust
The idea that I was capable was one she did not trust
How far would I have gone had she given me her all?
Had she just reached out her hand to me and not just let me
    fall?
I guess I'll never really know, but I know it's not too late
I have a brand new teacher now who has not sealed my fate
She says that I can do it; we work until I do
She's patient and determined. She believes in me. Do you?

7

Meting Out the Seating

A Point to Ponder

 When you go with a friend to a movie, or to a play, or to a ball game, whom do you sit next to? Do you pick out the strangers and sit next to them, or do you prefer to sit next to your friend? We know the answer, of course. Why is it that you choose to sit next to the person you know? We'll answer that for you. You want to sit next to your friend because you feel more comfortable being next to someone you know, because you can converse with your friend, and because it's just more fun that way. That's just human nature. Now, let's say that you are at the movie theater with your friend and someone comes into the theater right before the movie begins and announces, "That's it. Everyone, listen to me. I am going to tell you where to sit. And I want to ensure that no one is sitting next to anyone they know or will be tempted to talk to, because you aren't supposed to talk during the movie!" Just imagine it. Now, as an adult, you may even leave the theater at this point. If nothing else, you will be upset. Again, that's just human nature.

Can you see where this is leading? **On the first day of school, students walk into your classroom and want to feel as comfortable as possible.** So they select seats next to their friends, for the same reasons we just stated above. Oh, and they are definitely more apt to converse with someone they know than with a stranger. That, of course, could mean trouble for you, the teacher. Now, you have a choice to make. And most teachers think they only have two choices: (1) Let them sit where they choose and wait until behavior problems occur before moving them, or (2) assign seats and hope that they are not seated next to too much temptation. We believe there is a better, more effective way.

Classroom Solution/Strategy

On the first day of school, it is important that you don't immediately leave a bad taste in students' mouths. You want them to *want* to come back tomorrow. This is not to say, however, that you let the students run the show. Instead, we suggest that you let them choose their own seats on that first day.

We also suggest that you let them know that you want them to feel comfortable in your classroom, so you have decided to let them sit where they choose for a few days. Then say, "We'll talk about what happens after that later, but I know you'll like it." That's it. Don't give out any more information than that at first.

The fact is that within a few days, you will begin to notice that **some students are perfectly capable of sitting next to friends and not causing disturbances**. You will usually select only a few students who, for the sake of your sanity and everyone else's, will need to be separated. You will also notice students who are not the greatest of allies who have ended up much too near one another. Usually, most teachers will agree that five or six strategic "moves" will get things in order regarding seating assignments.

So now you need a plan for making these moves and keeping students happy. Before you think to yourself, "My job is not to make my students happy," then consider that happy students behave better and are more eager to learn and do their best. Happy students are more motivated. Happy students spread happiness to other students. Okay, you get the point. So how do you move a student who, because of his choice of seating in your classroom, represents imminent behavior problems? How do you do this and still keep him happy? You use a little psychology. Here's an example that one teacher shared with us:

> I had five or six students who needed to be moved to other seats in my room because of behavior issues. In one case, the student was too far back and I wanted him to be right up front. In the other cases, I needed to move students away from other students. But I didn't want to make it appear that I was punishing anyone. So I simply did the following: I told my students that I needed to make a few seating changes for *my* benefit. I told the one student who was seated too far to the back of the room that I wanted to give him the responsibility of picking up papers when students would pass assignments forward, and that in order for him to do that, I needed him to be seated in the front of the room. Not only was he willing to do it, but his behavior improved because I had given him some responsibility! I did this with each of the other students, too, assigning various jobs and seating them in places where their jobs could be best served. They bought it, and I had no problems. Since then, I have used that same approach for years with much success.

Another idea is to **use "cooperative grouping" as a way to arrange seating**. Tell your students that you will arrange the seating according to their groups. In other words, divide your students into cooperative groups (where you determine the group members and are careful about which students can and cannot work together), and then you can arrange the seating so that their desks are near their group partners for cooperative grouping time. They will never know that while you were doing this, you were also separating some of them from their "partners in crime." We suggest changing these groups every few weeks and letting the students know, in advance, that you will be reassigning groups often and thus their seating will be changing accordingly.

We are not suggesting that, if a problem is chronic, you should not talk to the student about it and change his seating assignment. But we think you will find that you will have to do this much less often if you're using some of the ideas we've provided above.

Bottom Line

 The bottom line is that the seating arrangement in your classroom does affect behavior. You will have to change your seating from time to time due to this fact. But you can save yourself much heartache in the process by using a little psychology. **By carefully meting out the seating, behavior problems you'll be defeating!**

8

Happy Notes to Parents

A Point to Ponder

Most parents want to believe that they are doing a good job raising their children. Most parents are proud of their little angels. Most parents become threatened and maybe even a little defensive if someone suggests that their child is anything less than perfect. That is, of course, because they think that a less-than-perfect child is a direct reflection of their less-than-perfect parenting. **Parents love nothing more than to hear something good about their children.** Also, most children want their parents and teachers to be proud of them. Now let's bring these facts into the classroom.

Classroom Solution/Strategy

The strategy we are about to share with you is used in countless classrooms, always with amazing success. Here it is: **Send one note per class per day—one "happy note," that is— to the parent/parents of a child in your classroom.** A happy note consists of wording along these lines:

> Dear _____, I am so proud of your child, _____, for
>
> _____
>
> _____. I knew you would be proud of her, too.

And that's it. Fill in the blanks, and sign your name. What many teachers do is photocopy these letters in order to have them ready at any given moment. Filling in the blanks takes all of about twenty seconds, yet its effect is far-reaching.

So let's say that you have a child who is behaviorally "challenged." We're sure you could find many reasons—legitimate ones—to write to her parents and give a litany of all that is wrong with this child's behavior. But before you do that, you may want to consider "catching" her behaving (as we'll discuss in more detail in #22) and seizing that opportunity to write a "happy note" to her parents. These kinds of notes almost always make it home and then onto the refrigerator! You were not dishonest as you did not claim that this child is always well behaved. Instead, you capitalized on a moment of good behavior and used it to help promote continued good behavior.

Now imagine that you send one of these notes, per class, per day to parents of your students. That means that every parent of every child you teach receives a positive note from you every month or month-and-a-half, depending on the size of your class. Even if it's every two months, that typically means more positive notes than these parents have ever received from their children's teachers!

Okay, so now you've established, through these notes, that **you are a teacher who notices good things about children and actually cares about the children you teach.** So when and if you ever do need to contact a parent about his child's misbehavior, he/she will be much more receptive to what you have to say. Again, no rocket science here. Just basic human nature!

Most importantly, **you will almost always see improved behavior from a student who notices that you notice good things about her!** This is a free and easy technique that will take, at most, one minute of your time, per class period, per day. This will be a minute well spent, as it will provide you with many more "minutes" of good behavior.

Bottom Line

 By sending "happy notes" to parents, you will enhance relationships with parents, relationships with students, student behavior in general, and your own mood! Free, effective, and easy. **So, as an antidote, write a note and gloat, and better behavior you'll promote!**

9

Their Own Notes to Parents

A Point to Ponder

 A little psychology goes a long way! For years, teachers have struggled with writing the dreaded "your child is misbehaving in my class" notes to parents. Usually the note expresses exactly what the child is or is not doing in class or what the child has done to someone else. This type of note sometimes gets "lost" in transportation or often lost in translation.

Dear Parent

Your child did something awful today while he was in my room
I hate to have to write this note, so filled with doom and gloom
But I must send it to you because I thought you'd like to know
And I'm hoping you can talk to him and punish him harshly—So
that he begins behaving now and causes me less trouble
If we don't nip this in the bud, the trouble may soon double!

Dear Teacher

I got your note and spoke to my son who said he did not do it
He says no matter what he does, somehow you misconstrue it
So behavior needs to change, all right, that behavior being your own
We'll expect that you apologize in order to atone!

Does the above interaction sound way too familiar? If so, we have a solution!

Classroom Solution/Strategy

Announce to your students that you will no longer write notes to their parents if they misbehave. This announcement will most likely be met with cheers and sighs of relief. Tell them, "Instead, *you* will write the notes. You are old enough and mature enough now, and I'm sure you would rather write that type of note yourself than to have me write it." Be cautious not to say this in a sarcastic tone, but rather act as if you are doing a favor for them. That's it.

Now, **the next time a student does something inappropriate and you want to let the parents know, have the student write the note.** Let's say that Susan calls Monique a "bad" word, and this has become somewhat of a habit for Susan. Simply say to Susan, "I know that you realize that your parents need to know about this, so go ahead and write a note to them telling them what happened." Tell her it's okay to write the "bad" word in the note. So Susan reluctantly begins writing:

Dear Mom and Dad,

In class today, I called Monique a _____.*

Love,
Susan

Teacher signature: _____

Parent signature: _____

---

*We're sure you can use your imagination to fill in the blank.

You, of course, sign it, and then you send the note home with Susan, telling her to return it the next day. You may be amazed to learn that you will never again have a parent contact you saying his child did not commit the act in question. That's because the child actually admitted it in her own handwriting. The note comes from the child, not from you. This, to parents, is much less threatening and usually more believable.

But what if Susan comes to school the next day and claims to have "forgotten" to give the note to her parents? There's a simple answer to that one also. You just make a phone call, with Susan right next to you, saying, "Mrs. _____, this is _____, Susan's teacher. Susan had a note to give you yesterday, and she forgot to give it to you. Instead of bothering her with bringing it home again, I'll just let her tell you what was in the note. Here's Susan!" And you hand the phone to Susan. This technique works like a charm. And usually students only have to experience this once before their behavior miraculously improves.

Bottom Line

 When a child clearly "admits," in her own words and in her own handwriting, to something she did, you escape being "accused" of over-reacting or falsely accusing the child of something she did not do or making a big deal out of nothing. Have students write their own notes to their parents!

If a child writes her own note to her mom or to her dad,
Admitting in her own words that she did something bad
Her parents will believe it, and although they may be mad
Behavior might improve even more than just a tad!

10

Make Them Responsible

A Point to Ponder

A little responsibility can foster a more responsible attitude! Yet, many teachers overlook this fact of life and neglect to spend time intentionally making their students more responsible.

Responsibility, by definition, usually implies being accountable to someone or for something. It also implies a position of authority. **Children and adults alike, when placed in positions of authority, will more often than not rise to the occasion.** Responsible people tend to behave more appropriately than do irresponsible people. Sometimes, if you give an irresponsible person a little responsibility, he will become a lot less irresponsible. But it is best to do this in small bites. Likewise, if you constantly remind an irresponsible person of just how irresponsible he is, chances are good that he will become even more irresponsible. So let's take those facts and use them to our benefit in fostering better behavior in the classroom.

Classroom Solution/Strategy

Although you are the ultimate authority in your classroom, and although we do not suggest that you give over your duties and responsibilities to your students, we do recommend that you gradually give your students more and more responsibility. We also recommend that you identify your *least* responsible students and get to work on them quickly!

A fellow teacher shared the following with us:

One of the very first things I do is to identify my least responsible students and start to make them responsible. I know that behaviors I focus on will expand

and those I ignore will diminish. So I try to assign duties to my students and set up the chance to point out just how responsible they are becoming. I even send notes home to parents telling them just how proud I am of their children for being so responsible. Even though I teach high school, I assign some of the very same jobs that my wife, who is an elementary teacher, assigns to her students. I make someone responsible for picking up homework. I make someone else responsible for erasing the board. I make yet another student responsible for passing out stickers, yes, stickers, to deserving students. I have to say that my wife is the one who gave me the idea, and at first, I didn't believe that it would work. But seeing that I have no problems with some of the same students that other teachers are having major problems with has made a believer out of me. As the school year progresses, I increase the responsibility, as my ultimate goal is to teach them that they are responsible for themselves. I find that the more responsible I make them, even with small tasks, the more responsible they become. And the more responsible they become, the better behaved they are.

Bottom Line

One of the most profound things that the above teacher said, in our estimation, is the fact that **what you focus on expands and what you ignore diminishes.** So focus on making your students responsible and their irresponsibility will diminish. When irresponsibility diminishes, good behavior improves. We simply cannot add to that!

11

Stress Success, Not Duress

A Point to Ponder

 At the risk of overstating the obvious, we ask you to consider the fact that success breeds success and duress breeds duress. But, obviously, this is not obvious. If it were, then all teachers in all classrooms would be stressing nothing but success in order to accomplish a common goal—making students successful. Research continues to show that there are many more negative statements spoken to students by teachers than positive ones. Further studies show that the human brain takes much longer to process a negative statement than it does to process a positive statement. And yet more research shows that while a student is processing negative thoughts, it is almost impossible for the student to learn. If this is true, then the solution should not be complicated. Wouldn't we want to stress success in our classrooms and not duress? Shouldn't stressing success be our primary focus as classroom teachers? Yet, in our own observations, we frequently hear many more negative statements than positive ones. This, of course, does not mean that all teachers are negative. **The very best and most effective teachers rarely utter a negative statement.** However, even they would be the first to admit that we can all work at being even more positive and stressing even more success.

Classroom Solution/Strategy

 We know of a teacher who is a master at stressing success in her classroom. She teaches at-risk students who have been retained several times in school, who have behavior challenges, who have been suspended and/or expelled from their previous schools, and who have not met with much success at all in school. Yet, every year, she manages to do two things: She gets them to behave and to succeed. What more could any teacher want? And she does it with students whom many of her coworkers would not want to teach. So we asked her to share her secret. Here's what she shared:

> These students have been labeled as "bad kids." Most of them have already been in trouble with the law. The average age in my seventh grade class is fifteen. And these students want to be anywhere else but school. So I have no choice but to make them successful and convince them that I believe in them. That's the only way they will believe in themselves. For instance, since most of them cannot write a complete sentence on the first day of school, and since I am supposed to get them to write structured essays before the end of the school year, I have to start from square one. I teach them, on the very first day of school, to write sentences that are so simple that they can all succeed. And then I praise them all profusely. When they see their successes, they are more willing to try again.

Now the fact is that within weeks, these students are writing much more complex sentences. Soon, they are writing simple paragraphs. And, finally, before the end of the school year, they are writing essays! To top it off, they are behaving far better than they were just a few months prior. And this teacher does it every single year! We have observed her in action many times, and we discovered the following secrets of her success:

- ◆ She smiles constantly.
- ◆ She expresses belief in her students, especially when they are finding it difficult to believe in themselves.
- ◆ She builds on their existing skills, never teaching "over their heads."
- ◆ She builds on every small success and continues to celebrate success, never duress, with her students.
- ◆ She knows how to scold a student in a nice way!

We actually attempted, during several of our observations of this teacher, to count the negative statements she used during any given lesson. Guess how many we found. None! And believe us, there were students in her class who could push anyone over the edge. This teacher, however, continues to keep her focus on making students successful. When asked about how she maintains such an upbeat, positive attitude in her classroom, she responded:

> There's just no room for anything negative with these students. Goodness knows they don't need yet another negative influence in their lives. So I don't allow myself the option of being negative, because I know it cannot lead to anything good.

Our suggested strategy for you is to do exactly what the above-mentioned teacher does. Make a conscious effort to begin stressing the successes of your students.

Bottom Line

 If you want a student to be successful, you have to set up a way to make him successful first and then build on that success. Continue to build on every little success every day that you teach. Remember that **if you begin to stress success, students will improve and not digress, and soon you will be seeing less of the misbehavior that leads to duress!**

12

Enthusiasm Breeds Enthusiasm

A Point to Ponder

Nothing is so contagious as enthusiasm.
Samuel Taylor Coleridge

Just as success breeds success, enthusiasm breeds enthusiasm. **Enthusiastic people are "contagious."** If you hang around them long enough, it's difficult not to catch their enthusiasm. Likewise, unenthusiastic people are also contagious. It's difficult to hang around them and not become depressed!

Observe a sporting event and notice the cheerleaders and the coaches. You will rarely spot one who lacks enthusiasm. Look into the stands and observe the enthusiasm of the parents, friends, and other spectators. Look onto the field or court and observe the enthusiasm of the players. Now walk down the halls of our schools. Do you sense the same enthusiasm? Sadly, in far too many schools and in far too many classrooms, you won't.

Classroom Solution/Strategy

We ask you to ask yourself, "Just how enthusiastic do I appear, every day, to my students?" If you are honest, your answer might be, "Not nearly enough." Since we, as teachers, take our jobs so seriously, we sometimes appear far too serious. Yet, we often notice that **the most enthusiastic teachers have the fewest behavior problems.** Now please don't misunderstand. We are not suggesting that you don't need good classroom management skills and ample content knowledge. You do. But an enthusiastic teacher who possesses average teaching abilities is far more effective than an unenthusiastic teacher who is above average on the competency scale. Ask any principal! Better yet, ask any student!

One of the oldest "tricks" in the book, shared by all of the great teachers, is that they always appear happy and enthusiastic. And whether they really are or are not, their students don't know the difference! Do these teachers always feel enthusiastic? No. Do they always appear enthusiastic? Yes! That, dear friends, is called professionalism.

As a simple, one-day experiment—in case you are doubting the effects of your enthusiasm on others—pretend to be enthusiastic in your classroom. Greet your students with enthusiasm and teach them with enthusiasm. Pretend that this day is the happiest of your life. We guarantee that you will see and feel a difference—a difference in your own attitude, a difference in the attitudes of your students, and a difference in the behavior of your students. In fact, we believe that this one experiment will be enough to make you want to become much more enthusiastic every day. Try it. You have nothing to lose and everything to gain.

Bottom Line

The fact is that your own enthusiasm will determine the level of your students' enthusiasm. And let's face it: If you can't feel enthusiastic around children, then you are in the wrong profession. Children are some of the most enthusiastic beings on the planet! So be enthusiastic and the difference will be drastic!

13

Pry for Why

A Point to Ponder

Somehow You Knew

I was struggling with a problem at home
And so, in class, my mind did roam
You asked if something was troubling me

And I said that I was fine
But somehow I could tell you knew
You saw inside my mind

Your actions said you understood
That you knew I was doing the best I could

And because of your understanding
I'll never ever forget you
And from this day forward, teach me *anything*
And I will let you!

It has often been said that if we knew the "reasons" behind the misbehavior of our students, then 9 times out of 10, instead of being angry, we'd be heartbroken. Yet often we become angry or frustrated; we dole out a punishment, and we dare students to misbehave again. But we forget the most important piece—finding out "why."

Classroom Solution/Strategy

We conducted an experiment with teachers and taught them the "Pry for Why" technique. This technique involves exactly what it implies. When a student misbehaves, hold your temper, maintain your control, and talk to him calmly. Ask him why it is that he acted in that way. Do this, of course, in a very sincere manner, and do it privately. Keep your frustrations out of it. If he mutters the famous student comeback, "I don't know," then simply say, "Well, think about it and we'll talk again a little later. You probably just need some time to figure it out." And always come back later and talk to him again. Usually, you will find that there is a definite reason for the misbehavior.

During our experiment, the teachers were amazed at the things they learned by simply prying for why. And, more often than not, they were heartbroken over what they heard.

Some of the students we teach deal with issues much too difficult for children to handle. No child should have to face some of the issues that some of our students face. But it's reality, so thank goodness for caring teachers!

Bottom Line

When a student misbehaves, there is usually a reason. And usually the misbehavior is a cry for help. When you know the reason, you can better provide that help and deal with the misbehavior in a way that will foster better behavior in the future. The "Pry for Why" technique is an easy, stress-free, effective way of doing this. **So we challenge you to pry for why!**

14

A Laugh is Half

A Point to Ponder

 The old saying, "laughter is the best medicine," is true. Scientific research continues to show that **laughter reduces stress, lowers blood pressure, helps the body to fight disease, and releases endorphins in the brain. Laughter also connects us to others in a positive way.** A good laugh makes us feel good and puts us in a better frame of mind. And when people are in a better frame of mind, their brains are better able to learn. When you are feeling happy, you are less apt to focus on the problems and stresses in life, which we all have.

Show us a classroom where laugher is prevalent, and we will show you a classroom where students are learning and behaving better than in one where laughter is absent. Regrettably, laughter is lacking in far too many classrooms.

We interviewed five teachers who had "laughing" classrooms and five who had "nonlaughing" classrooms. We asked one question: What do you feel about laughter in the classroom? Here are their answers:

1. "Laughter is vital in the classroom. It puts us all in a good mood and helps to make my classroom seem like a safe and happy place for my students."

2. "Teaching is serious business. Recess is time for laughing, but class time is for teaching."

3. "If I allow my students to laugh, they get carried away. It interrupts my teaching time."

4. "I have been teaching for over 20 years and have laughed every day of those years with my students. Students need to laugh. So do adults!"

5. "If you told me I couldn't laugh in my classroom, I'd have to quit teaching. I can't imagine a classroom without laughter. But I know of a few."

6. "Allowing laughter in the classroom is asking for trouble. It's hard enough to keep the students busy and serious, even in a serious environment."

7. "Laughter in my classroom is every bit as important for me as it is for my students. I love to laugh, and my students love it when I laugh with them. And despite what some teachers say, it is not true that laughter causes discipline problems. The very same students who are behaving in my classroom are causing problems in the classroom of one of my coworkers. She does not allow laughter, and the students resent that."

8. "I think laughter can be a good thing, but I'm afraid that if I let the students laugh, I may lose control. So I try to keep things on the serious side."

9. "I don't understand how some teachers can be so serious all the time. They're miserable, and so are their students. I love to laugh with my students. But they know when it's appropriate and when it's not, so it has never been a problem in my classroom."

10. "My students can't handle laughter. So it's really not an option for me."

Did you have any trouble determining which classrooms had laughter and which did not? To follow up on our interviews, we observed these teachers. In each of the five classrooms where laughter was prevalent, we saw the following:

♦ Happy students

♦ A happy teacher

♦ Enthusiasm for learning

♦ Good overall student behavior

♦ Motivated students

♦ A motivated teacher

♦ Students enjoying learning

♦ The teacher enjoying teaching

♦ A positive classroom climate

On the other hand, here's what we observed in each of the five classrooms where laughter was nonexistent:

♦ Unhappy students

♦ An unhappy teacher

♦ Lack of enthusiasm for learning

♦ Poor overall student behavior

- Unmotivated students
- An unmotivated teacher
- Students not enjoying learning
- The teacher not enjoying teaching
- A negative classroom climate

Taking what we know about laughter and about "laughing vs. nonlaughing" environments, let's bring that knowledge into the classroom.

Classroom Solution/Strategy

Look at the bulleted lists of what we observed in the "laughing vs. nonlaughing" classrooms. Now go into your own classroom and "see what you see." Note how often you and your students are laughing and having fun. We are not, of course, talking about laughing "at" students or condoning students laughing "at" one another. We know you know that. We are, however, suggesting that you begin laughing more, smiling more, sharing a few corny jokes, and making your environment more upbeat and happy! It's one of the simplest things you can do to improve student behavior.

An 86-year-old former teacher shared one of her secrets. She had spent 45 wonderful years in the classroom. She said, "I know I made more than my share of mistakes over the years, but I believe that one of my most important practices was to laugh with my students every day. I designated five minutes, every day, at the beginning of class, for joke time. I would share jokes and my students would share jokes. I established very clearly what types of jokes were appropriate and what types were not, so I never had a problem with that. In looking back, I think it's one of the things I'm most proud of, because I know how important it is to laugh."

Bottom Line

Fact: A good laugh is half the battle. If you can establish an overall positive classroom climate replete with laughter, you have just solved at least half of your problems! If you don't believe us, then you could use a good dose of laughter!

15

Student or Teaching Problem?

A Point to Ponder

Two teachers, Mrs. Pain and Mrs. Joy, are speaking to one another in the hallway before school begins. Mrs. Pain is complaining about three of her students: Billy the Bully, Larry the Lazy, and Mary the Mean. Mrs. Joy, who teaches these same students, remains silent. You see, she teaches Billy the Bright, Larry the Loving, and Mary the Mannerly. She simply cannot believe that these three wonderful students are even capable of causing the problems about which Mrs. Pain is complaining. Well, knowing Mrs. Pain, maybe she *can* believe it.

Why is it that the same students behave for some teachers and not for others? **The *same* students have been known to act differently in different classrooms.** When this happens, we know that we are not dealing with a *student* problem. There are two types of problems in the classroom: *student* problems and *teaching* problems. Notice that we did not say *teacher* problems, as we do believe that most teachers do the best they can with what they know. Yet, at times, some teachers mistakenly blame the students in such situations. The problem is that some do not know that there are some simple *teaching* strategies they can implement that will foster completely different and better behavior from their students.

The fact is that you cannot ever assume that a problem is a *student* problem unless you are sure of the following in your classroom:

♦ Procedures are evident.

♦ Organization is evident.

♦ Positive rapport with students is evident and the teacher appears enthusiastic.

- There is no *down* time where students have nothing to do.
- The teacher ensures success for all students.
- Lessons are well planned, relate to real life, and actively involve students.
- Every student is treated with dignity.
- The teacher does not allow students to push her buttons.

It is critical that you take a good look at this list and determine whether every one of these conditions is present in your classroom. If even one is not, then you must have it in place before you can determine whether your problems are *student* related. Many times, you will find that one or more of the above conditions are missing from your classroom.

Classroom Solution/Strategy

 Take the above list and *honestly* take a look at your own teaching, your own behavior, and your own classroom. Are any of these missing from your classroom? Let's say, perhaps, that you have your procedures set, that you are organized, that you are *usually* positive, that you keep your students busy from bell to bell, etc. However, every now and then, no matter how seldom, you react to a student's misbehavior. We didn't say you *deal* with it. We said you *react*. Maybe you sigh. Maybe you look up at the ceiling. Maybe you clench your teeth when you speak. Maybe you have an unusually large protruding vein in your neck. Get the picture? No one is pointing any fingers here, as almost all teachers have *reacted* to students from time to time. The problem is that this type of reaction has *never* worked. Ever!

Now take one of the listed items that is missing in your classroom and do the following: Using the aforementioned list, address one issue that is missing in your classroom. Even if you found three or four, select only one. For the entire day, address that issue. Let's say that you are not typically organized. Can you be perfectly organized tomorrow? No. Can you be better organized than you normally are? Yes. Our goal is not to help you become *perfect* but to help you become *better*. After you become better at this, move on down the list until you can ensure that all conditions are in place. But take it one step at a time. By doing this, you should see a marked improvement in student behavior!

Bottom Line

 In well-managed, organized classrooms, where teachers have positive relationships with students and work to ensure that students are actively involved and successful, behavior problems are minimal and are usually student related. And before you can effectively deal with a problem, it is important to be able to diagnose the cause of the problem. We've provided you with a road map for determining the causes of problems in your classroom. If you use it and determine that a problem is teaching related, make an adjustment in order to help solve the problem. If you determine that the problem is student related, deal with the student. **But remember that one of the most effective ways to change a student's behavior is to be in control of your own behavior and avoid reacting out of frustration.** Even in the most effective teachers' classrooms, a little change in approach on the part of the teacher can solve most behavior problems.

If She Can Do It, Why Can't You?

"Don't even think about it," you said
And so I just stopped thinking
"How many times must I tell you?"
I answered "50!"—without blinking
"Don't get smart with me," you said
So my studying, I stopped
When you said there was no hope for me
My bubble of restraint you popped

So no matter what you say or do
I'll be on the attack—and I'll get you
I'm not like this in my other class
—Don't you wonder why?
The answer is that my other teacher
Knows how to make me comply

She treats me with respect, you see
She believes I can and so I do
And so it simply baffles me
That if she can do it, why can't you?

Even when I make mistakes
She's figured out just what it takes
To make me behave and help me succeed
Her secret? Patience. So please take heed!
If you attack me, my resentment will breed
Your belief in me is what I need.

16

Learn What to Overlook

A Point to Ponder

There's a lot to be said for "picking and choosing your battles," especially in the classroom. Given the fact that students are children and children seem to require lots of attention, teachers have to determine what *kind* of attention to give and *when* to give that attention. The moment a student learns that he can get your attention, negatively or positively, any time he wants it, he will soon be vying for your constant attention and playing you like a fiddle! Therefore, you, not the student, need to be in control. And in order to be in control of when students get your attention and what kind of attention you actually give them, you will need to learn one of the great secrets of the most effective teachers—learning what to *overlook*, or at least pretending to overlook! You see, the most effective teachers sometimes use *ignoring* as a way of dealing with a situation. They realize that, in some instances, the best way to act is not to *react!*

Classroom Solution/Strategy

Too often, teachers stop the flow of activity—actually halting the entire lesson—to deal with one student. Sometimes, of course, this is appropriate. For instance, if a student is hitting another student, it is appropriate and necessary to stop what you are doing and deal with the situation. However, we continue to find that **more than half of all situations for which teachers stop teaching in order to address behavior problems could be better dealt with if ignored.** Here's an example: If a student is tapping his pencil on his desk in an attempt to get your attention, this is something that can usually be ignored. If you ask students to take out their books and only one student does not take out his book (again, in an attempt to get your attention), you may also choose to ignore this and see if he will eventually take out his book. But if you react and get upset, chances are good that he will fight back and will be more apt *not* to take his book out the next time and the next. Yet another example is a student drawing or doodling while he is supposed to be completing an assignment. Sometimes the best way to approach this is to redirect him instead of reacting to his lack of engagement in the activity. This can be done by asking him a question such as, "Billy, would you mind doing a favor for me as soon as you finish your assignment?" You may be amazed to learn how well this technique works. In essence, you appear to have overlooked the fact that he was not participating, but in reality, you simply dealt with it in a more effective manner.

The following are just a few examples of what the best teachers overlook:

♦ Student noises that are made to attract the teacher's attention

♦ Slouching in desks

♦ Daydreaming

♦ Underbreath comments designed to aggravate the teacher

♦ Slamming books on the desk when students are aggravated about something

♦ Less-than-pleasant looks on students' faces

♦ Occasional whispering between two students

♦ Occasional laughter between two students

Bottom Line

 If you look hard enough to find something wrong, you will find it every time! And if you stop every time all behavior is not perfect, then you may very likely never teach! So overlook what you can and deal with the rest. The skill of *picking your battles* will save you from war, and you'll promote the behavior you're looking for!

17

If You Sweat, They Win

A Point to Ponder

 Children are children. They are not young adults. They can be aggravating at times. None of this is news, is it? We all knew this when we signed on as teachers. Yet, we do tend to forget that our students are just children and they will act accordingly. Now, as children grow, they are supposed to learn to take control of their actions and reactions. That's when they become adults. But along the way, they need role models to show them what it looks like to be in control of oneself. So, because we are adults, we are supposed to be the ones providing that modeling. And to do that, we have to remain in control of our actions and reactions with children!

Don't Let Us Know

When you get angry, and you will
Be careful and then more careful still
Please don't let your anger show
'Cause if you do, then we will know
And once we know, that's it, you're through
You belong to us, not us to you
And once you're ours, we're in control
We'll never do what we are told
We'll push your buttons, we'll test your will
We'll never ever get our fill
So when you get angry, don't let it show
'Cause if you do, then we will know
And once we know, that's it, you're through
You belong to us, not us to you!

Classroom Solution/Strategy

By far, the biggest mistake classroom teachers make is they let their students know that the students have upset them. In other words, they lose control of their emotions. Thus, they lose control of themselves, period.

When students think they have *gotten you*, you lose every time. When they begin pushing your buttons, there's no stopping them. But wait a minute. Who showed them your buttons? You did. You have to know a button is there before you can push it. And the problem begins when we show our students that we have buttons that can be pushed. Solution? You cannot let your students know that you even *have* buttons! Students have to think that you are one of those teachers who just does not have any buttons. Once they think that, they will soon go to some other poor unsuspecting teacher down the hall for their thrills.

So what do you do when a student really aggravates you and leans on your *very last nerve*? You maintain a calm, composed demeanor and deal with the misbehavior in a rational, controlled way. This is what the great teachers do, every time. They always appear to be in control, and thus they have very few behavior problems. Don't misunderstand. The great teachers are every bit as human as their less effective coworkers, but they know the secret of hiding their buttons from their students. Is it easy? No. Is it effective? Every time!

The same holds true when a student asks you an inappropriate question and catches you off guard. When this happens, the student usually knows what he is doing and is trying to make you sweat. So what do you do when a student asks a question that is simply not appropriate for him to ask or for you to answer? Simply reply with the following question: "Why do you ask?" What you did was answer a question with a question. You did not look shocked. You did not seem upset. You did not sweat. You simply answered a question with a question. Works every time!

Bottom Line

The second a student sees you sweat, the game is on! He will do whatever it takes to make you sweat more often and more profusely. Thus, you cannot, for any reason, let your students know that they have personally offended or upset you. Hold them accountable? Yes. But do it in a calm, composed way. Become one of the great teachers who simply do not have buttons, at least as far as the students are concerned. Stay high and dry, and never let them see you sweat!

Remember, please don't let your anger show, 'cause once you do then they will know, and once they know, that's it—you're through. You belong to them, not them to you!

18

Defuse the Bully

A Point to Ponder

There's almost nothing worse for a student to experience in school than the all-too-familiar and much-dreaded encounter with the class bully. Oftentimes, children suffer in silence regarding their encounters with bullies because of embarrassment, a belief that they caused the bullying to occur, or fear of repercussions by the bullies. Consequently, teachers must be vigilant in monitoring bullying in the classroom and on the school grounds.

There are numerous reasons that some children bully others. Sometimes, children who bully have been bullied at home, so it's a learned behavior. At other times, it is a cry for help. Sometimes, it is a need to feel powerful over others, possibly in an attempt to regain the control they may be lacking in other areas of their lives. At times, it may be gang related. Regardless of the reason, **it is a form of aggression that is inappropriate and should not be tolerated.**

A keen awareness on the part of a teacher will play a key role in helping to lessen the effects of bullies and bullying behaviors. If the bullying is not addressed, bullies can become like rock stars, developing a following of their own. And, needless to say, discipline problems ensue. **Teachers must nip this problem in the bud by being aware, addressing the problem with both the bullies and their victims, and using techniques to help defuse bullying behaviors.**

Classroom Solution/Strategy

One of the simplest ways to help defuse the problem of bullying is to conduct a class discussion on bullying. The best time to do this is early in the school year, ideally before any bullying behaviors have occurred. In doing this, you are providing students with an awareness of and strategies for dealing with this potential problem. Talk about bullies and discuss, with the students, what it feels like to be bullied by others. Discuss why they think some people pick on others. Discuss the fact that victims of bullies should not blame themselves. Show them some ways to help defuse a potentially explosive situation. For instance, sometimes the best thing to do is walk away. At other times, it is appropriate to maintain eye contact, but always in a calm manner. **Although it is not always easy to maintain control while someone else loses control, adding fuel to a burning fire will never help to extinguish it.** When bullying occurs, it is appropriate (and should not be construed as tattling) for the victim and/or anyone who witnesses the bullying to share the problem with a teacher. The teacher can then determine a course of action and decide if people such as a school counselor, an administrator, or a parent should become involved.

Discuss the fact that bullying behaviors, if not addressed, will often worsen, so it is best to try to deal with these problems as soon as they begin. A role-playing activity, with students of all ages, can be a useful tool when learning about dealing with bullies. The school counselor can often participate in and/or facilitate the discussion and activities.

What you are doing, in essence, is bringing the subject to the forefront, being open about the fact that it can be a common problem and helping victims of bullies to know that they are not alone in their feelings and experiences. Through this type of discussion, students will learn that almost everyone has been bullied at one time or another.

We are not, however, suggesting that if one student is bullying another, that you suddenly invite the whole class to discuss it. In such a case, we suggest that you talk to both the bully and his victim separately. Of course you will try to get to the root of the bully's behavior and then help him to see the error of his ways, providing him with more appropriate ways of dealing with his feelings. As we mentioned before, administrators, parents, and/or school counselors are sometimes brought in to help deal with the problem effectively. On the other side, you have the victim, whom you will deal with separately and privately. Always privately! **We continue to find that far too many teachers wait until the bullying has not only begun, but escalated, before they jump in and try to deal with the problem. It is time well spent to address the likelihood of such a problem *before* it occurs.**

Bottom Line

 Although we are not suggesting that there is any "quick fix" for dealing with bullies, teachers can help to defuse aggressive behavior by doing the following:

♦ Discuss it before it happens.

- Provide suggestions for possible victims of bullies.

- Notice behaviors that border on aggression and deal with them immediately.

- Once the behavior has occurred, talk to the bully, attempt to uncover the reason for the behavior, and help the bully to devise ways of dealing with his feelings in an appropriate, nonaggressive manner.

- When appropriate, involve the school counselor, administrators, parents, etc.

- Deal with the bullies and their victims separately.

- Help the victim to see that he did nothing wrong, as victims of bullies often blame themselves.

- Help all students to understand that if they witness bullying, they should report it.

- Remain vigilant in order to protect all children in your care.

When the bully no longer pushes his weight, discipline problems soon abate!

19
Hold Private Practice Sessions

A Point to Ponder

 When a student does something inappropriate in class, he is usually expecting you to react in a certain way. He knows he has an audience (his classmates), and he is often putting on a performance. If you do what many teachers do and deal with him in front of his audience, the behavior will rarely improve. In fact, a bad situation will usually become worse. But **when you deal with even the toughest of students one on one, in private, most of the toughness fades away.** One of our favorite ways to break a student (of any age) of an inappropriate behavior pattern is to use the following strategy.

Classroom Solution/Strategy

 Talk to the student privately and say, "I noticed that you are having trouble remembering our procedure for raising your hand before speaking. Don't be too hard on yourself for forgetting. I'm an adult, and I often forget things. But I know how embarrassing it can be to forget so often in front of your friends. So here's what I'm willing to do for you. Don't thank me now, but I will give you my recess today and practice with you so that you will be really good at the procedure and won't forget so much. I'm happy to do that for you. See you at recess." That's it. In essence, you are pretending that you think that the student is just forgetting to raise his hand. Surely he would not be ignoring the procedure purposefully! The key is that you are not at all sarcastic and that you tell the student you are willing to give of your own time to help him. Do you see what you just did? You did not take his recess from him, but rather you gave him yours!

So the student comes in at recess and you say, "Thanks for coming in. Okay, now pretend that we are in class and you have something you want to say. Show me what you'll do." The student slowly raises his hand and you say, "Great! I can give you 15 more minutes of practice. Do you think you need more practice or do you feel you have it now?" The student always says, "I have it." Then say, "Great. See you tomorrow. Oh, if you forget again tomorrow, that's my fault. That simply means I didn't give you enough practice. I'll even stay after school for you if you need. Just let me know."

Now please note that this technique takes less than a minute, so the good news is that you do not lose your recess. And if you teach in a school where there is no recess, you can use this technique between classes, during your planning period, during lunch, etc.

When the student next returns to your class, be sure to catch him *not* talking and thank him. But if the problem becomes chronic again, simply have another private practice session. You can use this for virtually any sort of misbehavior.

One final note is that some teachers ask, "Well, what if the student does not show up at recess?" Our answer is simple. Go and find him and say, "Oh, you must have forgotten that you and I have a practice session. Let's go." And you do this with a smile on your face.

Bottom Line

The *private practice session* strategy is a simple one that produces amazing results. Anyone who tells you that private practice sessions with students don't work has obviously never tried them. Practice makes perfect, doesn't it? So practice, practice, practice, and watch behavior improve, improve, improve!

20

Speak Awfully Softly

A Point to Ponder

 Consider the fact that the **louder we speak, the less others listen.** A loud voice seems to collide with a brain's desire to listen. In the classroom, it is no different. We often notice that in great teachers' classrooms, their voices remain soothingly calm and pleasant. That is because they know that when they speak softly, others seem to feel that what they have to say is important. Thus, others listen. In the classrooms of less-than-effective teachers, we continue to notice that their voices tend to be much louder. Soft voices tend to express caring. Loud voices tend to express aggravation and agitation.

That is not to say that there is never a need for a loud voice. If you are coaching from the sideline, you definitely need to raise your voice in order for the players to hear you. If a child is about to run out in front of a moving bus, you scream as loudly as you can! But in the classroom, teachers' voices are best and most influential when calm and soothing.

Consider the following scenario: A student is upset and expressing anger toward another classmate. The confrontation is escalating, and the student's anger is building. His voice is getting louder. Enter the loud teacher.... The teacher begins to scream at the student, telling him to stop it and to calm down. But nothing about the teacher's actions is conducive to ending a confrontation. Nothing about the teacher is calm. The teacher is actually fueling the flame. This never works. The fact is that a calm, professional approach is the only way to calm an angry student. The louder he gets, the softer you become, period. This works with adults, too, by the way! Fires require fuel to burn. Don't feed the fire!

Classroom Solution/Strategy

 The best way to gauge your volume level in the classroom is to start listening to yourself. Notice how loud your voice is or is not. If you need, have a coworker or administrator sit in the back of the room, just for a few minutes to provide you with some feedback as to your volume level. You might even choose to video yourself so that you can actually hear how you sound. The key is to find a level that is calm, pleasant, and only loud enough to be heard by everyone in the room, regardless of where you are standing.

Another thing that effective teachers do is that they tend to lean forward while speaking, their body language expressing that they have something really important to say. They don't lessen their level of enthusiasm, however. They simply express their passion for teaching and enthusiasm for learning in a calm, soft voice.

When faced with a confrontational student, effective teachers remain calm. Their voices remain soothing, though serious. They speak with the student, rather than scream at him. Oftentimes, they tell the student that they will give him a few minutes to cool down, and then they will speak with him.

Bottom Line

 A soft voice portrays a calm demeanor. A calm demeanor is contagious. **Calm environments are environments that are conducive to good student behavior.** So speak awfully softly!

Your Silent Voice

I had a temper tantrum—a shouting, screaming fit
You calmly walked away from me
You left and that was it
I wanted you to scream right back
And fuel my burning rage
To forget you were my teacher
And act like one my age
But you weren't even fazed
Or at least you didn't show it
I tried to leave you dazed
But you won, I lost, I know it
And maybe you already know
That because of the restraint you show
The lesson in your silent voice
Will help me make a better choice.

21

Teaching in Small Bites Makes Them Hungrier

A Point to Ponder

 When faced with a task, we usually accomplish more by taking one step at a time. With any task, if you look at only the end result, you can soon feel overwhelmed. But if you look at only a small step at a time, the task can seem much more doable (see #39). For instance, let's say that you have a party to host for a friend's birthday. If you look at the fact that all of the responsibility falls on your already-overburdened shoulders, you may soon find yourself stressed and overwhelmed. When you feel this way, it is difficult to accomplish anything. But if you realize that you have one month to plan for this party, and you plan small steps to accomplish every day, you may find that not only can this be doable, but you'll actually find yourself enjoying it and feeling highly confident and successful!

How do you put together a 500-piece jigsaw puzzle? One small piece at a time. How do you read a book? One page at a time. How do you eat an enormous banana split? One delicious bite at a time! **How do you make your students feel successful? By teaching everything you teach in small, accomplishable tasks, one bite at a time.**

Classroom Solution/Strategy

! Let's say that your students have to complete a project telling all about themselves. This project must include stories, photos, artifacts, and the like, all arranged in a specific format that you have devised. The project will take time to complete, so you will allow the students an entire month.

Teacher A gives her students a large packet of information early on a Monday morning. She tells them that they have one month to devise an "All About Me" project, and she then tells them everything the project will entail. The students appear, at first, curious. As she goes through four pages of explanations, they soon lose interest. Some are looking at each other as if to say, "What? I have to do all of this? No way!" By the end of her very long explanation, they all appear overwhelmed. Thus, their appetites have been spoiled. They don't like this food, and they are not eating it! By the way, she never shows them an example of what the finished product will look like! She then opens the floor for questions, which soon turns to a griping session. She becomes visibly frustrated, and so do the students. The only good news, to the students, is that they have a month to complete it. Many, of course, will wait until the very last week or even the very last night before the project's due date to even begin. Their parents will be angry; they will be angry; their teacher will be upset that the project is not complete; the grades will be bad; and you know the rest of the story.

Teacher B greets her students on a Monday morning by saying, "You are going to be so excited when you see what we'll be working on next." She has a former student, Michael, enter the room with a beautiful, colorful poster in his hand, entitled "All About Me." The student then proceeds to tell the class he will be sharing something he created last year in this very classroom. He tells about himself, about his family, about his interests; and he even shares a funny story about himself on a trip he took last year to an amusement park. After he finishes, the students applaud. The teacher has been successful in whetting the appetites of her students! The teacher then allows them to come closer, a few at a time, to view the project. While they are doing this, she is walking around placing a one-page instruction sheet on each student's desk. After thanking Michael with one last round of applause, the teacher tells her students that they will all be working on this with her guidance, one step at a time. No one complains. In fact, they all seem quite excited. They are now "hungry" for more! She continues to guide them, "feeding" them only one small bite at a time. It is important to note that students are given choices along the way. Since all students are not poets, then all are not expected to write a poem about one of their personal experiences. But writing a poem is one of three choices given for that particular step of the project. For each step of the project, the teacher has already planned for accommodating individual differences, thus providing choices as just described. In Teacher A's instructions, no such choices were given. By the end of the month, all of the projects are completed, and all students receive passing grades. Some are hoping that they will be selected to share their projects with next year's class, just as Michael did with them.

In #36, we address the fact that **some tasks, for some students, are not accomplishable, even in small bites!**

Bottom Line

 The fact is that teaching in small bites makes your students hungrier. It's easier for an unfit person to jog a block than to run a mile. And if one block is too long, he might begin by jogging ten yards. Regardless, if he begins by jogging a little at a time, consistently, he may eventually be able to cross the finish line. He might never win a trophy for being the fastest or the best, but he will be able to accomplish the task nonetheless. And so it is with students in the classroom.

Like a great chef, a great teacher serves her lessons in several courses, each course to be savored and enjoyed before leading to the next. Feed them well and they'll always come back for more!

22

Saving "Gotcha" for Behaving

A Point to Ponder

 In the classroom, we tend to see more of what we encourage. We'll say that again: We see more of what we encourage. It is a fact that in the classrooms of great teachers, there is constant encouragement and very little discouragement. The very best teachers always "catch" their students behaving, thus discouraging the students who are misbehaving. They know what to ignore and what to notice.

We observed a wonderful teacher who had the skill of catching students behaving. She said, "I always save my 'gotcha' moments for catching students behaving." She was introducing a procedure for getting the students' attention. On the first attempt, several students did not follow the procedure. But instead of singling out the students who did not follow the procedure, she said, "Wow! Almost everyone got it right on the first try. You guys are amazing!" She then tried it again, praising, yet again, the students who were following the procedure. By the third attempt, all but one student was following the procedure. She pretended not to see him and moved on. Her choice to ignore that student was a very effective strategy. You see, that student wanted to push that teacher's buttons. He wanted her to notice that he had not followed the procedure. She, of course, was way ahead of the game and would not give him that kind of satisfaction! It's not like she was ignoring a student who was hitting another student. That, of course, would not be wise.

We continued to notice, throughout her entire lesson, that she made a concerted effort to catch students following procedures, paying attention, participating in activities appropriately, etc. The misbehavior that she intentionally ignored was minor. She was blind (or so the students thought) to all but good behavior; thus her classroom was filled with well-behaved students.

She shared with us the fact that she does, of course, deal with misbehavior, though she said she was careful about picking her battles. She explained, however, that when she deals with a misbehaving student, it is always done in private.

In far too many cases, we see teachers using "gotcha" for misbehaving students. In an observation of one such teacher, we observed the following "gotcha" moments:

- The teacher intentionally called on a student who was not paying attention during an oral reading exercise; and when the student did not know where to begin reading, she said, "Well, how *could* you know? You haven't been paying attention!"

- The teacher spotted a student whispering to another student while the students were completing a worksheet. She said, "Did I say to talk while completing your worksheet?" This was said loudly enough for the entire class to hear.

- The teacher, while collecting a homework assignment, noticed that all but one student had completed the assignment. Instead of at least noticing the students who had done what was expected of them, the teacher chose to single out the one student who had not completed his assignment, and then she chastised him in front of the entire class.

- While orally going over the answers to the aforementioned worksheet, the teacher called on a student who answered incorrectly. The teacher said, "Where were you when we discussed this earlier?"

This teacher, obviously, did not know the skill of saving "gotcha" for behaving. In fact, during the entire observation, she never caught one student behaving. Instead, she remained ever vigilant for all that was wrong.

Classroom Solution/Strategy

 Our strategy is simple: For one day, **intentionally use your "gotcha" moments only for students who are behaving**. If during this time a misbehavior occurs that simply cannot be ignored, deal with it privately. During this entire day, make a concerted effort to acknowledge appropriate behavior and to thank students for kind acts, valiant efforts, etc. The more you do this, the more you will notice just how well it really does work. We hope that this convinces you to use this strategy every day!

If you are someone who typically does notice and praise good behavior, then make an effort to do so even more. **As long as your praise is genuine and appropriate, you can never provide too much of it!**

Bottom Line

 Save your "gotcha" moments for good behavior and you will foster more good behavior. **We all like for our good deeds to go noticed!** Save your reprimanding, when it is necessary, for a private place and time. Even when misbehavior must be addressed, it should never be done so in a "gotcha" sort of way. We will address this further in the #23, where we find what's gleaming and redeeming!

23

Find the Gleaming and Redeeming

A Point to Ponder

A speaker stood in front of his audience and had them look around the room for everything they could find that was any shade of blue. He gave them thirty seconds to do this. He then had them close their eyes and remember as many things they could that were any shade of white. Most audience members could not think of a single thing that was white. In actuality, there was much more *white* in the room than there was *blue*, but most people could not remember anything that was white, and some of them were actually wearing white! The fact is that they were focusing so intently on finding blue objects that they never noticed the white ones! Moral? **Life is what we focus on! And so it is in the classroom.** If a teacher focuses on misbehavior and all that is negative, then that is what he will see. If he focuses on all the good going on in the classroom—and there are many good things going on in every classroom—then that will become the focus for everyone.

Classroom Solution/Strategy

For starters, choose one of your classes and make an effort to *notice one gleaming and/or redeeming trait in every student in the class.* Write it down, just in case you may forget. Next, point it out to the student. For instance, you may say to one student, "I notice that you always have a smile on your face. Some days when I'm not in the best of moods, I can always look your way and count on your smile to lift my spirits." To another student you may say, "I've noticed that no matter how much you struggle to understand the work at times, you never give up. We all struggle from time to time, but many people give up too easily. You've got what great people are made of! I predict that you'll accomplish great things in your life." Sometimes it may be something as simple as, "Thanks for holding the door for me. I appreciate that." The point is to start "focusing" on what's gleaming and redeeming in students—*all* of them! Start with one class and, if you teach multiple classes, spread the good cheer to all of them!

So what's the downside to using this strategy in your classroom? There is none. By focusing on what's good, you will see more of what's good.

Bottom Line

 As *teachers*, because we are trained to spot problems and fix them, we sometimes lose sight of all the good going on around us. We are so adept at spotting misbehavior that we sometimes place way too much of our focus on what is wrong. We catch our students misbehaving, but we often forget to catch them behaving. So turn that pattern around and start focusing on what's gleaming and redeeming in every student. By focusing on what's good, you will diminish and sometimes eliminate the not-so-good. As an added benefit, your actions will help students to start focusing on what's right with them as opposed to what's wrong with them. That, fellow teachers, will almost magically foster better behavior every time!!! **So, hocus pocus, change your focus!**

24

Join the Ranks of Thanks

A Point to Ponder

Praise is one of the most valuable gifts we can give and receive. And one of the nicest things about it is that every time we praise someone, at least two people feel better—the one who received the praise and the one who gave it! If you have ever been on a diet, what is it that keeps you going? Is it when people say how good you look, or is it when people tell you it's about time? The praise, the fact that someone notices and recognizes your efforts, is what you will more likely appreciate and what will motivate you to continue on your diet.

This same approach is used by effective teachers, on a daily basis, to motivate students and enhance good behavior. These teachers know that the behavior they notice and acknowledge will always be the behavior that is repeated. They know what students they can praise publicly and what students tend to be embarrassed by such praise, so they also use anonymous public praise. Rather than singling that student out by saying, "Thank you, Johnny, for getting quiet," an alternative approach involves saying something like, "Thank you, class, for getting quiet." This way, the ones who were doing it (including Johnny) think you were talking about them, and the others who were not have been reminded of the appropriate behavior in your classroom.

Classroom Solution/Strategy

 One of the simplest ways to praise students is by saying "thank you," recognizing something they have done that was praiseworthy. It's a simple phrase that goes a long way in showing that you noticed a good behavior, saying that you appreciate that good behavior, and expressing that you value the actions of the student, thus valuing the student as a good person. Students who feel valued by their teachers tend to behave better.

We notice that **in the classrooms of effective teachers, the phrase "thank you" is uttered often, much more so than in the classrooms of less effective teachers.** We also find that in classrooms where teachers use the phrase "thank you" often, students also use the phrase more often than they do in the classrooms of less effective teachers.

Here are a few ways to use the phrase "thank you" in the classroom:

- ♦ Thanks, everyone, for entering the class so quietly. I really appreciate that.

- ♦ Susan, thanks so much for remembering to do your homework. That was very responsible of you.

- ♦ Simone, I love the way you take such neat notes.

- ♦ Eddie, thank you for getting busy on your assignment so quickly.

- ♦ Thank you, Linda, for staying in your seat today.

- ♦ Rebecca, that's an excellent story. I can tell you put a lot of effort and creativity into it.

- ♦ Thanks for closing the door, Eric.

- ♦ Thanks, class, for working so well in your groups.

- ♦ Thanks, in advance, for picking up around your desks before the bell rings. I always tell the custodians that they hardly need to come in and clean the room because you are all so thoughtful about cleaning around your desks before you leave each day.

- ♦ Lisa, thank you for helping Liz with those problems. I know she appreciated it, but I wanted you to know that I appreciate it, too!

Please remember that it is never appropriate to use the phrase "thank you" in a sarcastic manner. Here is an example: The teacher says, "Thank you, Richard, for being quiet," while she is staring at Danny, who is talking. *Sarcasm never works!*

Begin to notice how many times you do/do not use the phrase "thank you" in your classroom. Even if you use it quite a bit, as long as it is genuine, you can never say it too often, so begin thanking your students even more than you already do. If you find that you do not say "thank you" very often, then begin to incorporate it into your daily conversations with students. Practice using it until it becomes a habit.

Bottom Line

 Thanking students for good behavior can go a long way toward building relationships. It also goes a long way toward enhancing good behavior. **So join the ranks of thanks and reward all of the good behavior in your classroom.**

25

Humiliation Breeds Retaliation

A Point to Ponder

 Think back to a time, in school, when you were humiliated by a teacher. Sadly, it has happened to most of us more than once. Remember what it felt like then. Our guess is that your memory will be vivid and unpleasant, even today. Do you now remember the teacher who humiliated you as one of your favorites? Of course you don't. In fact, **most adults will admit to still harboring feelings of resentment and dislike for teachers who humiliated them many years ago.** They can still conjure up the same feelings as if the act of humiliation happened yesterday. That's how powerful and damaging humiliation can be. No one ever says, "Boy, when Mrs. Crabapple humiliated me, it surely made me want to be a better student. I thank her for that even today. What a lovely gesture her humiliation of me was!"

Now Mrs. Crabapple may have argued, during her days of humiliating students, that her tactics got her students to behave. And maybe she was right in that the talking stopped at that moment or that the misbehavior ceased, at least for a time. What Mrs. Crabapple did not realize was that **humiliation never works. In fact, it causes resentment and embarrassment, and it often leads to retaliation.** Humiliated students often feel something like this: "Oh yeah? You might have gotten me to stop talking by embarrassing me in front of my friends, but I'll get you back!" And retaliation, on the part of a student, can have many faces, none of which are pretty.

Oh, and when a student retaliates after being humiliated, the teacher is usually appalled, thinking, "How dare he!" We are not, under any circumstances, condoning retaliation on the part of anyone, but we *are* asking a simple question: Who started it?

Classroom Solution/Strategy

The solution here is to take note of your actions and ask yourself if you are ever prone to intentionally embarrassing students in front of others. Do you single out students who are not paying attention so that everyone else can be made aware of that student's lack of attention? Do you speak to a student about a poor test grade in front of others? Do you ask for public apologies when a student has misbehaved in front of his peers? The list is endless, but we believe we have made our point. If you realize that you use any form of humiliation with your students, please reconsider.

There simply is no justification for humiliation. It is our belief that the humiliation of students by teachers is a form of *bullying*. Teachers are students' role models, and good role models never act like bullies. We have yet to meet a truly effective teacher who uses humiliation as a form of behavior management.

Bottom Line

We do want students to behave, of course. And throughout this book we share many ways of getting them to behave, but always with strategies that maintain their dignity and that allow you to maintain your professionalism. **Don't ever allow yourself to "bully" your students with humiliation. You can get them to behave without ever losing your professionalism** and without ever putting them on the spot.

Will I Ever Take a Risk Again?

My teacher explained some math to us
I pretended that I knew it
But I know that when I take the test
I won't know how to do it
With a spur of the moment decision
I didn't raise my hand
It wasn't worth the embarrassment to say
That I just didn't understand
'Cause yesterday another kid
Admitted he didn't know it
My teacher was really angry
And she didn't try not to show it
And everyone else started laughing
When she put him on the spot
So will I ever take a risk again?
In this class, definitely not!

26

Beware the 90/10 Rule

A Point to Ponder

 The 90/10 rule says that ninety percent of all discipline referrals are made by ten percent of all teachers. That's right, ninety percent of all students sent to the office are sent by only ten percent of all teachers. If you question that, ask a few principals to predict which teachers will send the most students to the office *next* year! They can do it, and they can do it accurately, proving that the 90/10 rule exists. Truly effective teachers rarely send students to the office. However, when an effective teacher does have to send a student to the office, the administrator takes it seriously.

When a teacher sends students to the office for minor offenses, such as not turning in homework, making funny noises in class, being aggravating, not paying attention, or a host of other reasons which could have and should have been handled in the classroom (not the office!), that teacher is admitting to the students (and to the people in the office) that she is incapable of handling typical classroom problems. Therefore, when the ill-behaved student returns to the classroom, he knows that his teacher cannot handle him. He is in control, because he knows how to make his teacher (the adult) lose control. So his bad behavior continues and usually escalates. And, usually, the teacher blames the principal for "not doing anything" when she sends students to the office.

Is there a solution? There is. Let's take a look at what effective teachers do.

Classroom Solution/Strategy

 Effective teachers have very specific techniques they use to avoid sending students to the office. **The first thing they do is to handle practically all misbehavior on their own, without having to seek help from the office.** They accomplish this by having good classroom management, treating all students with dignity, engaging students in their lessons, teaching from bell to bell, and basically using all *50 ways to improve student behavior* that we discuss in this book. Effective teachers know how to spot potential problems and nip them in the bud before they escalate. They realize that they, not their administrators, are in control of their own classrooms. So, at all costs, effective teachers do everything within their power to avoid sending students to the office.

But aren't there some situations where an effective teacher must send a student to the office? Yes there are, but these situations are rare. Thus, the 90/10 rule. However, many effective teachers employ a very clever strategy for sending students to the office in a "must do" situation. The strategy involves having the students send themselves to the office! Here's how it's done.

On the first day of school, when the teacher is introducing the students to the most important rules and procedures for the class, the teacher says, "And just so you know, I don't send anyone to the office for misbehavior." The students usually cheer upon learning this wonderful news. The teacher then says, "Now you might send yourself to the office." Looks change from elation to inquiry. The teacher then says, "The office has a couple of rules of its own, and if you break one of these, you will send yourself to the office. For instance, one of the rules of the office states that if any student is involved in a physical confrontation, he must send himself to the office. I'm sure you don't have to worry about that happening to you, but if it does, I'll do my best to make it easy on you and I'll go ahead and fill out the paperwork for you." So when it does happen that a student hits another student, the teacher simply says, "Douglas, I know you realize that you are sending yourself to the office, but why don't you just calm down for a moment and I'll go ahead and fill out the paperwork for you."

Do you see what has happened? The student has to take responsibility for his own actions! Wow! And the teacher has nothing to do with it, with the exception of helping Douglas by filling out all of the tedious paperwork for him. Ask teachers who use this technique if it works, and they will tell you it works like a charm!

Bottom Line

 In an effective teacher's classroom, the bottom line is that the students are told, in advance, from day one of school, exactly what actions will send them to the office. So discipline referrals have nothing to do with the teacher's anger level or frustration level with a student. They have only to do with breaking specific rules. No surprises. Students know to expect certain consequences for certain actions. If they go to the office for breaking a specific rule, they are responsible, not their teacher. How often do students go to the office for misbehavior in the classroom of an effective teacher? Barely and rarely! Join forces with the ninety percent of teachers who almost never send students to the office. It's a great club! Become the president!

27

We Care About Those Who Care About Us

A Point to Ponder

One of the most effective ways to improve student behavior is to convince students that you are on their side and that you truly care about them. We continually notice that **when students believe a particular teacher cares and is not *out to get them*, their behavior improves dramatically.** Conversely, when students believe that a particular teacher does not care about them or like them, they tend to view that teacher as the enemy, thus fighting back to protect themselves. We also notice that far too many teachers do far too little to convince their students that they actually *like* them!

Think about someone you know who really dislikes you but whom you like a lot. Having trouble? That's because it's almost impossible to like someone whom you believe does not like you. The same holds true in the classroom.

One of the most advantageous moments to convince a student that you care about him is the moment he misbehaves or does something inappropriate. Yet, far too often, teachers turn this opportunity into a negative experience, expecting positive results. A student misbehaves and the teacher immediately reacts in a negative manner, using one of a variety of techniques that has always, and will always, produce negative results. For instance, if a student is talking out of turn and a teacher singles him out in front of his peers, he will almost never stop the behavior. Oh, he may stop the behavior for a few minutes, but he'll usually return to the same behavior soon afterward. Publicly reprimanding a student, embarrassing him in front of his peers, is not a way of expressing caring and concern. Therefore, even though the student's behavior is inappropriate, he will almost never feel remorse or the need to change his behavior if he does not believe that his teacher cares about him. The following technique is a wonderful way of expressing caring and concern while dealing effectively (almost magically) with misbehavior.

Classroom Solution/Strategy

 In #4, we share a technique we call "Are You All Right." This technique is a wonderful way to express caring and concern as opposed to anger or sarcasm. We take it just a little further in the following scenario.

A student is misbehaving in your classroom, and you take him out and, like in #4, ask if he is all right. But make sure you tell the student that you care about him. Note some of his good qualities so that the student knows you notice and appreciate him as a person. Here is an example: After asking if the student is okay, say, "You know, Marlin, I really do care about you. You're a natural leader. I notice the way others listen to what you have to say, and I notice the way you don't take advantage of people. And since the way you were behaving in class was so inappropriate, especially for you, I knew something had to be wrong. I don't like what you did, but I do like *you*. So if you need a listening ear, you've got mine. So why don't we just erase the slate and go back into class and start over."

The technique takes all of about 30 seconds and produces amazing results. The student walks away feeling that you care about him and are concerned about his well-being. Isn't that what we want for all of our students to believe?

Bottom Line

The fact is that teachers who express caring and concern for their students have far fewer behavior problems than teachers who do not do so. When students believe you care, they tend to reciprocate with better behavior. So **convince them that you care and behavior problems will be rare!**

28

As Nice, Polite, and Motivated as YOU?

A Point to Ponder

Wouldn't life be grand if our students were as nice, polite, and motivated as we are? Are they? Given the fact that students' attitudes and actions in any given classroom often tend to mirror those of their teachers, maybe we should take a closer look at just how nice, polite, and motivated we really are.

Classroom Solution/Strategy

The strategy here is to determine just how nice, polite, and motivated you are. This will give you a baseline from which to improve and grow. Ask yourself the following questions, and answer truthfully:

- ◆ Do I smile most of the time in the presence of my students?

- ◆ Am I consciously nice to my students—all of them—on a daily basis?

- ◆ Do I take extra care to be a constant role model of courtesy in all situations?

- ◆ Do I appear enthusiastic and motivated while I am teaching?

- ◆ Even when I have to reprimand a student, do I do it in a calm, controlled manner, treating the student with dignity?

- Am I respectful at all times?

- Do my students think of me as a happy person?

- Does each student know that I like him/her?

While looking at the questions, did you find one or two areas where you might be a tad lacking? Even if you feel that you exhibit all of the above qualities on a daily basis, make an effort to become even nicer, more polite, and more motivated.

Please do not worry that, if you are too nice, you will become a pushover and the students just won't behave. As long as your students are clear on your classroom expectations and as long as you remain consistent with those expectations, you can be very nice and still foster good behavior. **The very best teachers are also some of the nicest people you will ever meet!**

Bottom Line

 Students respond best, behaviorally and academically, to teachers whom they view as nice, polite, and motivated. An added bonus is that they soon begin to mirror these very same behaviors. A frightening thought is that in the classrooms of teachers who are less than nice, polite, and motivated, these very same behaviors tend to be mirrored in their students. So become as nice, polite, and motivated as you would like for your students to be, and they may just become every bit as nice, polite, and motivated as you!

29

Unmask the Mask

A Point to Ponder

 Every student has a story. Although we try to get to know our students, we usually don't ever fully learn each student's story. **Every good behavior and bad behavior has a reason, a reason that stems directly from each student's story.** Some of our students have far too much tragedy within their stories. Some of our students see and experience things that no child or adult should ever experience. *Ever*!

Every teacher, from time to time, forgets that **there is *always* a reason when a student acts a certain way.** Sometimes the reason does stem from something that happened in class, but many times it does not.

From time to time, every student wears a mask—a mask to hide what's really there. Sometimes what's really there, behind the mask, is simple shyness; sometimes it is fear; sometimes it is deep pain; and many times it is repressed anger. Regardless, it is often difficult for such students to trust adults. Thus, they put on their masks. In the classroom of effective teachers, however, masks are not worn for long.

Classroom Solution/Strategy

 There are three steps that teachers must take in order to uncover the many and varied masks of all of their students. First, **teachers must realize that students wear masks!** Second, **teachers must always try to see behind those masks.** And third, and most importantly, **teachers must *never* take student behavior personally.** As we stated earlier, it is our firm belief that if we knew the "stories" behind the behaviors of our students, then nine times out of ten, instead of being angry we'd be heartbroken. Effective teachers follow the three aforementioned steps, first and foremost. And, along with these, they prove, through their daily actions, that they are trustworthy, caring, professional people who would never do anything to harm, embarrass, or belittle a child. Thus, they earn the trust of even the most distrusting students.

Bottom Line

 We believe that the following poem says it all.

Behind the Mask

If you could see inside of me, then surely you would know
That beneath my bad behavior is a kid who needs you so
I need to feel your love for me—I need your caring smile
I need to be important each day, if only for a while
I need for all your wisdom to pour out onto me
It might not sink in right away—but one day it will, you'll see
I need a lot of patience—I need a calming voice
I need someone to show me how to make a better choice
I know it won't be easy—I'll push and test you often
But surely, teacher, you must know that hard hearts can be softened
So see me as your challenge, your calling and your task
And search until you've found the good that's hidden behind the mask.

30

Don't Let the Mood Brood

A Point to Ponder

 Paul walks into class, obviously in a bad mood. Mrs. Ignore-Ya sees that he is not in a good mood, but she ignores him. "He's always in a bad mood," she thinks to herself. "He just wants my attention, and I'm not giving it to him." Paul puts his head down and does not do his work in class. His mood gets worse, and Mrs. IgnoreYa gets mad. A confrontation ensues.

Paul walks into class, obviously in a bad mood. Mrs. DontYaDare sees him, recognizes that he is in a bad mood, and says, "Don't you dare bring that attitude into my classroom, young man. Leave your anger at the door!" Paul thinks to himself, "You have no idea what I'm going through. How dare you be so rude to me when I'm already in a bad mood!" Paul slams his books on his desk, and Mrs. DontYaDare begins to fuss at him. He argues back, and it's all downhill from there.

Paul walks into class, obviously in a bad mood. Mrs. ICare, who is, of course, greeting her students at the door, recognizes his mood immediately. She gives him a caring look and says, "Are you okay?" He tells her he is not, and she says, "You look like you are upset, and I'm so sorry to see that. I'm here for you if you need to talk. You just let me know if you feel you're too upset to do your work, and you and I will walk out of the room and talk about it." Paul thanks her, walks into the room, sits down quietly, and gets busy doing his work. Mrs. ICare walks over to him and whispers, "Paul, I'm really proud of you. The fact that you were able to come into the room and get busy, despite the fact that you are upset, shows a great deal of maturity." Paul thanks her and continues working.

Classroom Solution/Strategy

Mrs. IgnoreYa's way of handling the situation only made matters worse. There are times when ignoring a student's behavior is appropriate. This was not one of those times. Paul needed someone to notice that he was upset.

Mrs. DontYaDare's approach, though different from that of Mrs. IgnoreYa, also made the situation worse. Paul was already angry, so becoming angry with him for being angry was disastrous.

Mrs. ICare knew that **allowing Paul's mood to brood could only lead to trouble**. Aside from that, she genuinely cared about Paul, as she genuinely cared for all of her students. So she spotted the problem and dealt with it, immediately, in a caring way. She calmed him by showing him that she noticed he was upset; she cared that he was upset, and she was willing to speak with him if he needed to talk about what was upsetting him. Then she expressed her pride in his maturity.

Bottom Line

When a student enters your classroom upset, don't ever allow that mood to brood. It will only make a bad situation worse. Students need to know that we care about them. Be a Mrs. ICare and behavior problems will soon be rare!

31

Who's the Most Positive?

A Point to Ponder

 Everyone knows who the positive people are on every faculty. The students know, the staff knows, the faculty knows, the administration knows, and the parents know. Do *you* know? Answer this question: Who is the most positive person in your school? Take a few seconds and come up with an answer. Picture that person in your mind. Now think about why you selected that particular person. How does that person treat you? How does that person treat students? What type of expression do you see, in your mind's eye, on that person's face?

Okay, now what is the name of that person? We hope you named yourself. Did you? If not, why not? If you did not name yourself, then you are not nearly the effective teacher that you are capable of being. You are not nearly the effective teacher that your students deserve. If you *did* name yourself, then congratulations! We challenge you to continue to be the most positive person in your school. But even if you did not name yourself, the good news is that **you can become the most positive person in your school tomorrow!**

Classroom Solution/Strategy

 Since we know that students respond best to positive role models, and since we, as teachers, are possibly their most important role models aside from their parents, then we have a responsibility to them. We have a responsibility to be the best we can, the most positive we can, the most influential we can.

Our task is huge, and it is not a simple one. It is, however, one of the most worthwhile tasks that anyone in any profession will ever undertake—that of influencing young lives and touching the future.

So take your task seriously and become the **most positive** person in your school! Smile often, have a kind word for everyone you meet, and teach with enthusiasm. Resist the urge to gossip and never take a student's behavior personally. Be the teacher your students deserve.

Bottom Line

The fact is that your **students need to think you are the most positive person they have ever known**. Do they?

The Happiest Teacher

Who is the happiest teacher
The most professional in my school
If I can't honestly say it's me
Then surely I'm a fool
For any effective teacher
Knows, for sure, one thing
Students want happy teachers
More than anything
So I'm starting to be happy today
And when looking back, my students will say
Of all the teachers I ever knew
The happiest one of all was you!

32

Become Interested in Their Interests

A Point to Ponder

Students who believe their teachers are interested in them as *people* are much more likely to behave than students who believe the opposite. Convince a child that you care about him, value him, and actually find him interesting, and he will be much more likely to find your class interesting and much less likely to misbehave.

One way to convince a student that you care about him is to get to know his interests. What does he like to do? What fascinates him? What are some of his after-school activities? With some students, their interests involve sports. Others may have hobbies. Many students have the opportunity to participate in extracurricular activities, but not all are so fortunate. Regardless, all students have their own sets of interests. Yes, *all* students are interested in *something*. Now your job is to find out what that *something* is.

Classroom Solution/Strategy

The most obvious way to find out what interests your students is to ask them. Hold discussions that allow them to share their interests with you. Another popular way of finding out what interests your students is to give them an interest inventory. These inventories are very popular with teachers because the students get to share what they love to do in writing; and then the teachers can keep these, study them, and decide how best to incorporate this knowledge into lessons and/or discussions with the students. Yet another way to find out what interests students is to observe them. Their actions will tell you a lot about them. If Mary is always off on her own reading a book, you have possibly learned two things. You have learned that Mary may not be comfortable in social interactions with others, and you have learned that Mary loves to read. Now you can ease Mary into some social situations and help her to feel more comfortable, and you can become interested in the kinds of topics she loves to read about, maybe even suggesting some interesting titles for her to consider. If Dan is often seen acting bossy with others, you may have just discovered his desire, though inappropriately channeled at the time, to be a leader. Now you can help to ease him out of his bossiness and move him toward leadership. If Tom loves skateboarding, ask him to tell you all about it. You can incorporate skateboarding into his writing assignments, into a physics lesson, and into any area of the curriculum. Another way to show your students that you are interested in them is to attend after-school activities. Attend an occasional sporting event or dance recital or band concert, etc.

As a final example, we will share this story that a very effective teacher shared with us.

> Marlo was a student who was quite withdrawn socially. Her teacher struggled to find what interested Marlo. Marlos's interest inventory was basically blank, and when asked what she liked to do, her answer was usually, "Nothing." She had trouble even making eye contact with anyone. Her schoolwork also left much to be desired. The teacher knew she had to break through, so she began to study Marlo closely, looking for clues about what interested her. Soon enough, she observed that Marlo was exceptionally neat. She arranged her belongings very neatly, constantly straightening items in and around her desk. The little work she did in class was always done in a neat handwriting. When she erased something, she was careful to make certain there was no sign of the erasure. Bingo! The teacher talked to Marlo one day and said, "Marlo, you have got to be the most organized student I have ever met! I marvel at your ability to keep everything about yourself and around yourself so neat and ordered. I would love to learn about how you do that, and I could really use your help." To make a long story short, Marlo became the teacher's interior decorator for the classroom. She helped her teacher to organize all aspects of the room and made many useful suggestions. She and her teacher began to discuss shows on television where professional organizers went into people's homes to do the very same thing that Marlo was doing in the classroom. Needless to say, Marlo was willing to come out of her shell when she realized she was interesting and useful to her teacher.

Bottom Line

The bottom line is that students like and need to feel that their teachers find them *interesting*. Convince a student that you like her and find her interesting, and you've forged a connection. **When students feel connected to their teachers, they achieve more and behave better.** *Very interesting!*

33

A Favor as a Lifesaver

A Point to Ponder

Fact: Almost *all* students enjoy doing a favor for the teacher and/or running an errand. Is this merely because it affords them the opportunity to leave your classroom? No. When a teacher asks a student to run a special errand or help accomplish some special task, it makes the student feel important. **And *all* students (and all people) like to feel important.** Yes, it may also feel like a tiny *vacation* to be able to leave the classroom. And no, not all students can be trusted to "wander the halls on their own" running errands, but *all* students should be provided an opportunity to do a favor for the teacher from time to time. Remember, doing a favor for the teacher does not always mean leaving the classroom. Favors inside the classroom might involve getting a student to move a chair from point A to point B, sorting a stack of papers, sharpening pencils, and so on.

Sometimes, you just need to give a student *breathing room* or time to cool off if he is upset about something. At other times, you may just need to help a student to feel important and responsible. Regardless, a favor can be a lifesaver from time to time!

Classroom Solution/Strategy

A very simple strategy for "creating favors" is as follows: Have an agreement with the teacher right across the hall. Tell that teacher that from time to time you may need to get a student out of your room for whatever reason, and if you do, you will send that student across the hall with a sealed, empty white envelope. The student, of course, will never know that the envelope is empty, as it will be sealed. So keep a stash of empty, sealed envelopes in a drawer in your desk. When you need to get a student out of the room, use one of your empty, sealed envelopes. The teacher across the hall will thank the student for delivering the envelope and watch as the student walks back into your room. That's it! Very simple and very effective.

Here is an example of the strategy in action: Marcus is upset, mumbling under his breath, not doing his assignment, and looking as though he is lighting his own fuse, which is about to ignite. You need to get him out in the hall so that you can talk to him about it. However, if you ask him to step outside with you, he may refuse, given his current state of mind. You simply walk to your desk, grab one of your empty, sealed envelopes and say, "Marcus, would you do a favor for me and take this to Mrs. Barker across the hall? Thanks so much." He gladly leaves the room. When he returns, you are out in the hall waiting for him. You then say, "Thanks so much for delivering that important message for me. But before we go back to class…" and you talk to him about the problem, with calm and concern.

Here is another example of the strategy in action: Rebecca is one of those students who is *slow to get started* on her work. You want to create an opportunity to praise her for getting started on an assignment quickly, but she never provides the opportunity for you to do that. A favor is about to be your lifesaver! You give the students an assignment, and you immediately go to Rebecca and say, "Rebecca, I want you to run an errand for me. As soon as you finish your work, let me know, so that you can deliver something for me to another teacher." Almost always, Rebecca, given the current circumstances, will immediately get busy on her assignment, if for no other reason than to run the errand. She does not know that you are using this opportunity to set her up for success. As soon as she finishes the assignment, you send her to deliver one of your empty white envelopes. When she returns, you say, "Thanks so much for delivering that important paper for me. Thanks, also, for getting busy so quickly on your assignment. Have you noticed that you're getting better at that? Do you mind if I write a quick note to your parents and tell them I'm proud of you?"

These are merely two examples, but we feel sure that once you attempt this strategy, you'll find many more ways to *create favors* that will suit the needs of both you and your students.

Bottom Line

- Students like to feel important.
- Almost *all* students like to run errands or do favors for the teacher.

- Teachers can use *favors* to provide a student with time to cool down, to help a student to feel important, to create an opportunity to praise a student, and for many other reasons.

- A favor can be a lifesaver for both students and teachers from time to time.

34

Admit Your Mistakes

A Point to Ponder

 As teachers, we all set goals for ourselves, and we all have an idea of the kind of teacher we are striving to become. If one of your goals is that you aspire to be the *perfect teacher*, we advise you to run from teaching! Run hard, run fast, and do *not* look back! You see, there is no *perfect teacher*. Even the very best teachers make mistakes. But one trait that separates the best from the rest is that the best teachers are not afraid to admit their mistakes, even (and especially) in front of their students. Why is this? It's because they realize that **part of being a positive role model involves teaching students, through example, how to admit mistakes and how to use them as stepping stones to achievement.**

Classroom Solution/Strategy

 Consider the following scenario: Mrs. Right is writing a sentence on the board. She incorrectly uses *there* instead of *their*. Nick, an adept student, spots the mistake and points it out to the teacher. Because Mrs. Right is never wrong, she answers by saying, "Good, Nick, I'm glad you caught that. I did that on purpose to see who was paying attention."

And now consider this scenario: Mrs. I.M. Human is writing a sentence on the board. She incorrectly uses *there* instead of *their*. Luke, an adept student, spots the mistake and points it out to the teacher. Mrs. I.M. Human answers by saying, "You are absolutely correct, Luke. That's my mistake. Thanks for pointing that out to me." She corrects the mistake and then uses a *teachable moment* to hold a discussion on the proper uses of the words *their* and *there*.

Now **let's analyze the two scenarios.** Mrs. Right chose to *hide* her mistake from the students, leading them to believe that she had made the mistake intentionally. She chose not to take advantage of admitting a mistake in front of her students. Now isn't it true that some teachers actually do make mistakes (intentionally) to see if their students can spot the mistakes? Absolutely. The difference is that these teachers usually announce, "I'm going to make several mistakes in the sentences I'll be writing on the board, so pay close attention and see if you can spot the mistakes."

Mrs. Right, as a rule, never admits her mistakes in front of her students. In fact, when a student asks her a question to which she does not know the answer, she always responds with something like, "Well, I know the answer, but I want you to do some research and find the answer on your own. Telling you the answer would be like spoon feeding you." No student has ever caught Mrs. Right admitting to being wrong. Therefore, in Mrs. Right's class, students do not feel that it is okay to be wrong.

Mrs. I.M. Human took an opposite approach. She chose to serve as a positive role model by readily admitting her mistake to her students. She then chose to go beyond admitting her mistake. She used it as a teachable moment to reinforce the proper uses of *their* and *there.* In the classroom of Mrs. I.M. Human, students know that all people make mistakes, that it is okay to be human, and that it takes maturity to do the right thing and admit to those mistakes. Thus, students in Mrs. I.M. Human's class participate freely and do not feel intimidated by their own humanness!

Bottom Line

The bottom line is that we are all human—and **our students need to learn from our humanness.** Sometimes it's great to make a mistake and admit it to others so they can discover that being wrong and saying so can help them learn and help them grow!

35

Seeing Eye to Eye

A Point to Ponder

A speaker stood in front of an audience of teachers and intentionally looked right above their heads. He delivered his speech without ever making eye contact with the teachers. He also looked down and to the side. He scanned the entire room, but he never made eye contact. The teachers looked up, down, around, and back, wondering what he was looking at, knowing he was obviously not *interested* in them. Mild confusion led to bewilderment and then to disengagement. Once the teachers began to disengage, he began to make eye contact with those who were not paying attention. This, of course, made the audience very uncomfortable. Finally, the speaker admitted that he had played a trick on them. He had put them in the shoes of students in the classrooms of teachers where there is little positive eye contact. His point was to prove the importance of eye contact. "You see," he said, "teaching is a personal profession, built on human relationships. **If your students don't believe you care, they won't be interested in anything you have to teach."**

To be able to teach our students, we have to forge bonds with them, letting them know they are important to us. And **one of the best ways to tell a student that he is important to you is by making positive eye contact with him.** Also, by modeling positive eye contact—looking at a student intently as you speak with or listen to him (often accompanied by head nodding),—you are helping the student to develop the same skill.

Sometimes, teachers unwittingly teach to one area of the class. Their eyes seem to focus on the front of the class or the center of the class. Students on the *outskirts* of the teacher's comfort zone do not receive eye contact until they do something wrong. Then they receive the dreaded *teacher eye*. In such a situation, these students learn that eye contact is to be feared. Thus, they never make eye contact with the teacher. It is in this type of classroom that we often hear the surly phrase, "Look at me when I'm speaking to you!"

This, of course, is not an appropriate way of modeling the importance of eye contact.

Yet another common mistake stems from the fact that teachers are busy people. They are always doing something, and often that "something" involves looking at paperwork. A teacher is looking at a piece of paper intently and a student approaches with a question. The teacher answers the student's question without ever looking up from the paper. Big mistake! Yes, you are busy people, but never too busy to stop and make eye contact with every student who needs you. Be conscious of this in your own classrooms.

Classroom Solution/Strategy

Conduct an assessment of your eye contact skills. For one day, be aware of making positive eye contact with each student. Greet them as they enter, intentionally look at every student as you are teaching, look at each who asks a question or shares information, etc. If it feels a little *different* or *strange* to do this, then you have just learned that you need to work on your eye-contact skills. Also, be very careful to avoid *staring a student down* when you are angry or frustrated. You can look at a student in a serious way that expresses disappointment and concern without appearing angry and out of control. *Serious* eye contact is different from *negative* eye contact.

Even if you find that you are fairly good at making positive eye contact, there's no such thing as too much positive eye contact in a classroom. In fact, good eye contact is also a good discipline technique. Most students don't misbehave until the teacher is *not* looking at them. So look at them often and listen intently!

Bottom Line

The bottom line is that positive eye contact goes a long way toward building positive relationships with students. Negative eye contact goes a long way toward destroying relationships with students. Serious eye contact should not be confused with negative eye contact. So practice positive eye contact, and there will be no need for negative eye contact and fewer occasions for serious eye contact.

> Look at me and let me see
> That you're listening and you care about me!
> When I learn that you're genuine, then I, too,
> Will begin to look right back at you!

36

Bell-to-Bell Teaching

A Point to Ponder

A teacher shared the following scenario: "I remember it like yesterday. It was my first year of teaching, and I said to my students, 'We only have a minute and a half until the bell rings. If you can be quiet, I will not give you anything else to do.'" Chaos, of course, ensued, and the teacher became disillusioned, thinking, "You see? You can't even give them a privilege. They take advantage of it!" What the teacher did not realize was that this whole chaotic situation could have been avoided had she known this fact: If you give a student, of any age, ten seconds with nothing to do, he will find something to do *every time*! And it will almost never involve doing something constructive. This teacher learned a valuable lesson on that day—**teach from bell to bell, never allowing your students time with nothing to do!**

Classroom Solution/Strategy

How do you keep students busy from bell to bell? The simplest way is to plan activities that are not too lengthy. For instance, if you plan for a 30-minute activity, some students will finish in 15 minutes and some will take all 30 minutes or more. This will mean that many students have nothing to do. Teachers then resort to saying things like, "Read your library books." The most effective teachers plan brief activities that move quickly and involve all students. This is because they know that when students are busy, they are less likely to misbehave. They don't even give their students time to *think* about misbehaving. Lessons are paced so that one activity flows quickly into another. Students are discussing, problem-solving, working, acting, and doing.

Here are a few tips for planning activities that keep students busy and engaged:

- Plan for student-oriented activities that allow for student input and involvement.

- Plan for activities that are brief and that flow quickly into other activities.

- Structure your discussions to involve all students. Guide these discussions carefully so as to keep them interesting, inviting, and engaging.

- Plan for group activities where each student in the group has a specific purpose.

- Always plan an extra activity or two for "just in case."

- Always have a meaningful activity for any student who finishes an assignment early.

A teacher shared with us another simple way to plan for active student engagement. He said, "I started writing my lesson plans by beginning each sentence with, 'The students will....'" Wow! What a concept! Every single sentence in your lesson plan! Just begin each sentence with, "The students will..." and you will ensure that you are actively involving your students!

Bottom Line

 Active student engagement discourages student misbehavior.

Keep Me Busy

Busy, busy, you keep me busy
So much so, it makes me dizzy
Moving from one thing right to another
No time to think of anything other
  than the work I'm busy doing
Misbehavior has no time for brewing
Working, working all day long
No time for doing anything wrong
Questioning, answering, discovering, learning
There's an upward trend to the grades I'm earning
You keep me so busy and so engaged
I never have time to misbehave
Before I know it, the day is done
Learning, in your class, is really quite fun!

37

Smile, Smile, Smile!

A Point to Ponder

> ### To Smile or Not to Smile
>
> I am a brand new teacher
> Who's been told to hide my smile
> And it's clear that the teacher who told me that
> Hasn't smiled in quite a while
> With lines so deeply etched in her brow
> It seems that there's no turning back now
> Like her, I do not wish to be
> So I'm trying to ignore her advice to me
>
> And I notice that none of her students
> Respond to her very kindly
> They run out of her classroom each day
> When the bell rings, screaming "Finally!"
>
> So smile I will and successful I'll be
> A happy teacher my students will see
> For happy students behave, I'm told
> And miserable teachers grow miserably old.

Ask most new teachers you meet if they have ever been given advice similar to that in the poem, and they will tell you they have. But the simple fact is that telling any teacher not to smile and to appear serious most of the time is *bad* advice! Children need happy adults in their lives. They need to see their teachers smiling—often!

One main trait that sets the best teachers apart from the rest is that **the very best teachers smile most of the school day.** They realize the importance of being positive role models for their students every day. It does not mean they are any less human than their more negative coworkers. It does not mean that their lives are easier or that they always get the best and most well-behaved students, although their negative coworkers would refute this. It simply means they know how important it is to smile, even through the pain at times. They know how to appear professional, at all times, while practicing their chosen profession. They do not, however, smile at inappropriate times, such as when a student is misbehaving and needs to be corrected. But the fact that they smile most of the time absolutely decreases the times that students are misbehaving, as we will discuss in the following strategy.

Classroom Solution/Strategy

 Here is a *strategy* that the best teachers always implement: The best teachers know that **it is extremely difficult for a student to misbehave when his teacher is smiling at him. This is why the very best teachers smile most of the time!** Think about that. It is almost impossible to misbehave when someone is smiling at you! So yes, we are suggesting that the simple act of smiling can dramatically improve the behavior in your classroom. It's a free strategy that does not take any extra work and does not involve more or different lesson plans. It relieves stress, it enhances a positive learning environment, and it puts students at ease. Happy, calm environments contribute to happy, productive, well-behaved students.

How often do you smile at your students? Do you greet them each day with a smile? Do you begin each lesson with a smile? Do you encourage them with a smile? Do you thank them often with a smile? And is your smiling face the last thing they see as they leave your room each day? If not, you have some homework to do, but we believe that you can do it! It may take some practice, but we believe that you can do it! It may seem a bit awkward at first, but we believe that you can do it! There is absolutely no downside to smiling and smiling often.

Bottom Line

 We leave you with the following advice:

> Smile away and successful you'll be
> A happy teacher your students should see
> For happy students behave, we're told
> And miserable teachers grow miserably old!

38

Teaching With Urgency

A Point to Ponder

Have you ever watched a late-night infomercial? Have you ever purchased the end-all, be-all, magic product from one of these infomercials? Even if you haven't made the purchase, you have more than likely been tempted to keep watching. There are reasons these infomercials tend to hold us spellbound. One of the main secrets of an infomercial's mass appeal is its sense of urgency. You've heard it: "Order in the next twenty minutes to receive a special bonus!" "The first 500 callers will receive not one, but *two* of these amazing age-defying, gravity-reducing, wrinkle-erasing magic wands!" "But wait, that's not all...." Okay, you get the point.

We find that **watching a great teacher teach is a little like watching an infomercial!** Great teachers teach with a sense of urgency. They reel their students in with "teasers" and leave them wanting more, wondering what mysteries will be uncovered in tomorrow's lesson. They are storytellers, actors, salespeople, and infomercials all rolled into one!

Classroom Solution/Strategy

Making every day seem important is critical to having engaged and well-behaved students. Students are seldom late for (or try to skip) classes if they feel they might miss something of value. Begin each lesson with something like, "Just wait until you see the amazing things I have in store for you today," or "I can't wait to see how much you can accomplish during the next thirty minutes," or "I am so excited to teach this to you today, because we are going to have so much fun!" And, of course, you have to act excited! Just as we discussed in #12 *(Enthusiasm Breeds Enthusiasm)*, your excitement will become theirs.

Now, in contrast to what we have just discussed, imagine a scenario in which a teacher begins a lesson with a serious look on her face and says, "Open your books to page 134." There simply is no comparison. Too many teachers do not appear to *love* what they are doing, and their lack of enthusiasm spills onto their students.

Another strategy in teaching with a sense of urgency is to actually lean forward, like a coach coaching in the huddle, when you teach something new. Your body language must say that you are enthusiastic about what you are teaching. Your voice should do the same. You have to get excited first, regardless of the subject matter, and act as though everything you say and do is important and exciting.

Bottom Line

 It is critical for understanding and critical for good behavior that we teach with a sense of urgency. Become a walking infomercial and sell what you are teaching every day, leaving them wanting more and always anxious to return the next day. Sell when you tell and you'll reach them when you teach them!

39

Make it Doable and Chewable

A Point to Ponder

If you were asked to count the number of jelly beans in a jar, you could easily manage that task. As an added bonus, you might even enjoy sampling some of the wares. However, if you were placed in front of a swimming pool full of the sugary candies and asked to total the amount, you would probably not even attempt the task. Why? Because you would very likely feel that you could never complete the task successfully. And even if you could complete it successfully, it would take too long. And what if you lost count half way through? How frustrating! Far too often, students have that same feeling—especially if they are struggling learners. We put them in front of the *swimming pool* instead of in front of the *jar*, and they give up before they even begin! Worse yet, they give up on the task and resort to various modes of misbehavior to cover their lack of success. You see, the fact is that if a student can *count* the jelly beans in the jar, then he can very likely count the ones in the pool. The difference is that one task leads to success while the other leads to frustration. So the key is to make your assignments doable and chewable, ensuring a much better rate of success while still accomplishing the same objective. In #21, we addressed teaching in small bites – taking a larger activity and breaking it into smaller, accomplishable pieces. In this section, we will focus more on teaching at the student's level, making him successful one step at a time.

Classroom Solution/Strategy

Remember that **some tasks, for some students, are not accomplishable, even in small bites!** For instance, if a student cannot write a sentence, then teaching him to write an essay is pointless. He must learn to write a sentence before he can use many sentences to write an essay. Period! If a student can't add, then teaching him multiplication tables is pointless. He must know how to add before he can multiply. Period! If you try to teach multiplication to a student who cannot add, even in small bites, he will soon give up and may very likely become a behavior problem. So teaching in small bites, alone, is not enough. **Remember that the task, no matter how small, must first be doable.**

Breaking down a lesson into accomplishable parts can help engage every learner, including those who struggle the most. Give your students small, doable tasks. The length of these can increase as their skill levels increase, but never make any task too long. Small bites are easiest to chew!

This concept, of course, does not only apply to curriculum-oriented tasks. Effective teachers use small bites in all that they do. For instance, if they want a student to stop talking out of turn, they don't wait to reinforce his appropriate behavior until the end of the week. Instead, they set small, accomplishable goals at first. They start with one activity where the student is not allowed to talk out of turn for, let's say, a 30-minute period. Once the student is successful for 30 minutes, the activity is stretched to 45 minutes and then to an hour. Eventually, the student becomes successful at not talking out of turn for long periods of time.

Here is another example for making tasks doable and chewable. Let's say you want to increase student attendance. Don't wait until the end of the year to award perfect attendance certificates. By that point, you will have very few with perfect attendance. Instead, start saying things like, "Class, do you realize that this is the fifth day in a row that everyone has been here? This is amazing! It surely makes me feel fortunate that I am your teacher! Let's keep track and see if we can get to eight days in a row." Providing segmented chances for success can lead to a long pattern of accomplishment!

Bottom Line

No successful runner started by running a marathon. No successful skier started from the highest mountain top. Success comes from taking small, consistent steps toward a goal. Effective teachers make their students successful on a daily basis by making everything doable and chewable. **Just as, in eating, small bites are better for digestion, in learning, small bites are better for success!**

40

Brag About Them to Others

A Point to Ponder

One of the most powerful ways a parent can reinforce a desired behavior in a child is to brag about that child to another adult, in earshot of the child! One of the most powerful ways to stroke an employee's ego is to have him find out that you bragged about him to the boss! And the very same thing applies to the classroom. Want student behavior to improve? Brag about your students' good behavior to others, and do it in the presence of your students!

Classroom Solution/Strategy

When a visitor enters your classroom or the principal comes into the room, use this as an opportunity to reinforce positive behavior by saying something like, "This is the class I was bragging to you about. I am so proud of how they line up and quietly move to the lunchroom each day. And, they are a room full of outstanding readers!"

Hearing you brag about them to others goes a long way in building a positive bond between you and your students. It also increases the likelihood that the desired behavior will continue. Another approach you can use is to share with your students that you were recently bragging about them to someone else. Say, "I was bragging about you to the other science teachers yesterday, telling them that your biology projects were some of the best I have ever seen. I told them how attentive you all are to details and how well you work together in your groups to accomplish tasks." You might also share with the class that you were bragging about them over the weekend to your spouse, the principal, or even the superintendent.

Bottom Line

 Keep in mind that when bragging about your students in the past or present, you are really planting seeds for the future! By treating students as if they are already the people you want them to be, you are increasing the chances that they really will surpass the ones you bragged about!

41

The Diversion Excursion

A Point to Ponder

 Sometimes, the best way to change a behavior is to break a student's pattern. And one of the best ways to do this is to divert the student's attention. Parents do this all the time with their children. If a small child is whining about something he wants but cannot have, the parent will divert his attention to something else by creating a type of distraction. Many dentist offices play soothing music to divert the patient's attention from his fear of a possible painful experience. Flight attendants explain what passengers should do in case of an emergency in the air and then quickly divert the passengers' attention by offering music, in-flight movies (never those including airline mishaps), food, and beverages! Realtors divert our attention from negative details of a property by focusing on what a wonderful home this could be for us, focusing on all of the unique amenities, asking us to imagine ourselves living here in the lap of luxury! Investment experts focus on how much money we can make, rather than on the possibility of risk and loss. That is not to say that they don't warn us of possible risk, but the possibility of gain becomes the focus. All of these are what we will call *diversion excursions.*

If used appropriately, diversion excursions can act as lifesavers in the classroom. Effective teachers are masters at diverting students' attention.

Classroom Solution/Strategy

Monique is talking, while she should not be talking, to a fellow student. The teacher spots the talking right as it begins and chooses to use a diversion tactic by simply calling Monique's name. Monique looks up, thinking that she is in trouble. Instead, the teacher says, "Remind me that I have to ask you about something later. I might forget, so please remind me." That's it. Monique is not sure if the teacher has spotted her talking or not. Regardless, she will usually stop the talking. Later on, if Monique remembers to remind her teacher of whatever it was her teacher wanted to ask her, the teacher simply makes something up, like, "Was that you I spotted yesterday in the grocery store?" Monique says, "No, I wasn't in the grocery store yesterday." The teacher responds by saying, "Oh, then you must have a twin!" You see, the teacher just needed to create a distraction, but the student will never know that.

John gets up out of his desk, obviously on his way to another student's desk, and the teacher says, "John, are you on your way to the garbage can? Here, (as the teacher grabs a piece of paper) would you please throw this in the trash for me? Thanks for helping to keep our classroom so neat!" Where do you think that John goes? To the trash can. He never says, "No, I was on my way to hit Tim because he made an ugly face at me!" Again, another successful diversion excursion.

Bottom Line

In the classroom, sometimes the most effective way to deal with a potential or actual problem is to create a diversion, thus breaking the student's pattern. It's a simple technique that does not call attention to negative behavior. If handle it appropriately, the student never knows it even happened!

If you want an immersion of behavior conversion, simply embark on a diversion excursion!

42

Change the Way They Think

A Point to Ponder

 People usually don't change what they do until they change the way they think about what it is they're doing. You won't succeed on a diet unless you change the way you think about eating, be it choosing different types of foods you eat, different amounts of foods you eat, different times of the day that you eat, different reasons you eat, etc. You won't solve a problem you've been trying to solve by using the same three methods that have been failing to solve the problem. You have to think of a different approach, and in order to do that, you often have to view the problem in a different light.

A student who does not like a particular subject will never like it until he sees it differently. And that is where we, as teachers, factor into the equation. **Oftentimes, we have to change the way our students think about what we are trying to teach them before they will be able or willing to learn what we are trying to teach them.**

Classroom Solution/Strategy

 Let's look at different approaches to the same subjects.

Scenario 1: Timmy is in fifth grade, and he says he hates reading. Why does he need to read anyway? He's not going to be a reading teacher! His teacher tells him he needs learn to read because it's important in life. Timmy thinks his teacher does not know what she's talking about. He still hates reading, and that's that!

Across the hall, Tommy is in the fifth grade, and he says he hates reading. Why does he need to read anyway? He's not going to be a reading teacher!

His teacher asks him what he would like to become. He tells her he wants to be a race car driver. His teacher then convinces him that all race car drivers (and all drivers, for that matter) need to be able to read. They discuss reading signs, reading instruments, passing the driver's test, etc. He admits he's never thought about it that way. His teacher suggests a few books about cars that he may be interested in reading.

Now who has begun to think differently about reading—Timmy or Tommy? And who will very likely now *want* to read more?

Scenario 2: Susan's class is studying the Civil War. Susan has always maintained that she hates history. The activities this week include reading the chapter on the Civil War, answering the questions at the end of the chapter, completing four worksheets, watching a video, taking notes, and memorizing lots of dates, places, battles, and so on for Friday's test. The Civil War, to Susan, is simply a boring story in a book.

Across the hall, Sally's class is studying the Civil War. Sally has always maintained that she hates history. Sally's class is divided into cooperative groups where each group studies one aspect of the Civil War and then must determine how their lives would be different today had the Civil War never taken place. Students are working together, discussing, and learning that past events affect the present. Each group is given a set of instructions from which they must devise a presentation to be shared with the class. The Civil War, to Sally, was a meaningful event in history that helped to shape the world she knows today.

Now who has begun to think differently about history—Susan or Sally? And who will very likely now be more interested in studying events of the past?

Bottom Line

 The bottom line is that if a student sees no relevance in what he is studying, he will resist any attempts to learn what he is supposed to be learning. Convince him that what he is learning affects him personally, and he immediately begins to think differently! Thus, he actually *learns* what he is supposed to learn because you have changed the way he *thinks*. **One of our main tasks as teachers is to change the way our students think about learning** in order to make them hungrier for all the wonderful foods we have to feed them! Remember that many children won't eat broccoli unless you cleverly disguise it with cheese sauce! Become a gourmet teacher!

43

Nip It in the Bud

A Point to Ponder

The Andy Griffith Show is one of the most famous shows in the history of television. Almost anything you need to know about life can be learned from Andy and the gang from Mayberry. Although Sheriff Taylor portrayed the voice of calmness and reason, the most memorable character may be his legendary counterpart, Deputy Barney Fife. Although he represented the antithesis of calmness and reason, Barney was not without his wise moments, one of his most famous being, "You've got to nip it, nip it in the bud!" By this, of course, he meant that **it is very important to deal with small issues before they become big ones,** just as if you nip the bud of a plant, you prevent it from reaching full bloom. Let's take Barney's advice into the classroom.

Classroom Solution/Strategy

The most effective teachers agree that, on a daily basis, we have to "nip it, nip it in the bud," by ensuring that when minor problems occur, we address them before they become bigger problems or, worse yet, daily habits. **None of us want to see little annoyances become debilitating problems.** It is much easier to call a parent and ask for his help with a small behavioral or academic issue before it reaches full bloom than it is to have a conversation after you have reached your breaking point and the student's grades have fallen and/or the discipline problems have escalated. It is also much easier to have an immediate and private conversation with a student who walks into class appearing upset than it is to ignore it. Ignoring it will often lead to the student's acting on his upset feelings in an inappropriate manner. (In #16, we addressed learning what to overlook, and we listed examples of behaviors that can often be effectively overlooked. In this section, we are referring to issues that can lead to more serious problems and thus should not be overlooked.)

It is also essential that you make sure that your approach to a problem is not an escalator in itself. Stopping class and humiliating a child in front of his classmates will do little to nip it in the bud. As a matter of fact, this approach will most assuredly add more weeds to your garden!

Bottom Line

 Effective teachers know how to spot potential problems and nip them, nip them in the bud. This is why they have very few serious discipline problems. In actuality, they face the very same challenges that less effective teachers face, as they all deal with children. And children will act like children, much to the surprise, sometimes, of less effective teachers. Also, much to the surprise of less effective teachers, it's not that the effective teachers just "get all the good kids." The difference is that the **effective teachers nip buds on a daily basis, allowing only desirable, beautiful plants to flourish in their gardens of students.**

44

Discover the Beams of Their Dreams

A Point to Ponder

Here is a simple fact: *All* **students have dreams.** Here is another simple but sad fact: **Far too many teachers have no idea what their students' dreams are!**

An education consultant was called upon to help solve "the problem with the students" in a large, inner-city school. The consultant was warned that **the teachers were doing all they could, but the students just didn't care.** The school district, in a last-ditched effort, resorted to calling in an expert on student behavior. The consultant asked to observe each teacher's classroom. She also asked that each teacher be notified in advance of her visit, so that no one felt there were any surprise attacks. The consultant wanted to ensure that the teachers were showing their absolute best teaching, having had time to prepare.

And so the classroom visits began. In classroom after classroom, the worst misbehaviors observed were inattentiveness, student chatter, and occasional displays of disrespectful conversations, on both the parts of teachers and students. Regarding instruction, there was very little. In almost every classroom, activities consisted of reading chapters, answering questions, completing worksheets, copying notes, etc. How could the students be excited or engaged? In only one classroom was there excitement and enthusiasm demonstrated on the part of the teacher. And, not surprisingly, this teacher had no discipline problems. This was the teacher all the students loved. This was the teacher many other teachers despised. We will call this teacher Mrs. Happy.

Before leaving each classroom, the consultant conducted a discussion with the class, where each student was asked one simple question: **"What is your dream?"** To each teacher's amazement (except for Mrs. Happy, who already knew her students' dreams), each student had a dream, and each was willing to express, publicly, that dream! Most of these teachers later admitted that they had no idea that so-and-so wanted to be a veterinarian or a nurse or a coach or, yes, a teacher! Why did these teachers not know this? They had never asked. In the case of the student who wanted to be a veterinarian, her teacher was surprised to learn that the student volunteered her time, three afternoons a week, at a local veterinary clinic. The teacher said, "I didn't know she had it in her!" How could this teacher have known if she had never taken the time to ask?

Classroom Solution/Strategy

 Given the fact that you cannot teach a student until you reach a student, and given the fact that all but one teacher had not bothered to attempt to reach these students personally, it was no wonder that these teachers were struggling to teach their students. We won't even go into the fact that most of the classroom activities were noninstructional to boot!

Mrs. Happy, of course, knew all of her students' dreams. She had taken the time to get to know them, as people. She took personal interest in every student. She also planned lessons that actively engaged her students, and her students both participated and succeeded in her lessons.

So the simple strategy is to get to know your students and find out who they are as people!

Bottom Line

 Do you know your students' dreams? Do you know who your students are behind their textbooks and notebooks? Do they know you care? Do you make a concerted effort to show them that you value them as real people with real dreams? Be a Mrs. Happy, and discover the beams of their dreams!

45

Work that Body Language!

A Point to Ponder

 If you say, in an angry voice, "Well that's just great!" do you *really* mean that that's just wonderful? Of course not. But if you say, with a smile on your face and excitement in your body, "Well that's just great!" then doesn't it *actually* mean that you are happy and excited about whatever it is that is just great? (Same words, different body language.) Now shake your head back and forth as if to say, "No," but say the word *yes* while you are doing it. Does it send the message of "yes" or that of "no"? Hard to decide, isn't it? Imagine a mother looking at her son who just came out of his room dressed in his tuxedo for the prom, saying, "Look at you!" Now imagine the same mother looking at her same son who just walked into the living room covered in mud saying, "Look at you!" One of these times, the mother is happy, and the other time she is angry, but the words are exactly the same! That is because your actions speak louder than your words. So it is in life, and so it is in our classrooms.

Too often a teacher has a slight confrontation with a student. To the teacher, it is no big deal. She goes home and never thinks about it again. That is because the teacher could not see her own body language and was only thinking about her words. The student, however, didn't really hear her words because he was too busy reading her angry body language. The next day, one or two irate parents are waiting (in the office) for the teacher when she arrives at school. They begin by accusing her of saying things she did not say. Well, let's say she did not *speak* the words the parents are accusing her of having spoken, but her body language surely spoke those words.

Students "hear" our body language much better than they hear our actual spoken words. The most effective teachers know this, and they are *always* aware of their body language in the classroom.

If you're still not convinced, and if you happen to have a dog or have a friend who has a dog, go to the dog and smile and act very excited to see him and pat his head and say, with the most pleasant of tones, "Bad boy, bad boy." The dog will think he is being praised, because he is simply listening to your tone and reading your body language. The words you are speaking really mean nothing to him. With animals and with people, it's not so much *what* you say as it is *how* you say it and especially how you *look* when you are saying it!

And here's one more example: If a parent tells his child every day for ten years that honesty is the best policy and then lies only *one time* in front of his child, the child will take his cue from the action rather than the years of telling! The next time the child tells a lie and the parent punishes him for lying, the child will almost always say, "But *you* did it!" Any parent can attest to this fact.

Classroom Solution/Strategy

Our actions definitely speak louder than our words! The failure to realize this fact has been the downfall of far too many teachers. So the strategy here is to **accept the fact that your students are listening to your actions much more so than they are listening to your words.** This is why it is so important never to act when angry, never to let a student know he has pushed your buttons, never to *stare a student down.* These actions do not demonstrate control; they demonstrate *loss* of control! (See #50.)

The trick is to be aware, constantly, of your body language and be sure that you always possess the body language of a professional who is always in control. All of us, even the very best teachers, can improve on our body language in the classroom. Too many teachers appear far too serious while they're teaching. They forget how important it is to appear pleasant, always conveying the appearance that they love what they are doing and that they are in control of themselves, every minute of every day.

So **work on your body language.** Record yourself teaching and then watch the recording. No one has to see it but you. You will probably find that you don't appear as happy or enthusiastic as you were actually feeling while you were being recorded. While you watch the recording, count the number of times you smiled, count the number of times you used positive comments with students, and watch the responses from your students. You can learn a lot by doing this. But even if you are not brave enough to watch yourself on tape, at least become aware, every day, of your actions.

Bottom Line

 Because your actions speak louder than your words, and because students are watching every move you make much more so than they are listening to your every word you speak, **decide to make your tone more pleasant and your actions more positive.** Students respond better to positive teachers, and they behave better in the classrooms of these teachers. *You* set the mood in your classroom every day! Set a good one!

46

No Rest for the Weary

A Point to Ponder

 How many *off* days (bad days) are surgeons allowed? We are not referring to vacation days, but rather to days when the surgeon is allowed *not* to do his best in the operating room. None, right? We surely hope so. How many *off* days are airline pilots allowed? You know, the days when it's okay for them not to be paying attention at the controls. None, right? And now, how many *off* days are teachers allowed to have in the classroom? We're assuming you've answered, "None." But isn't it true that we've all known teachers who have more *off* than *on* days in the classroom? These are the teachers you greet by saying, "Hi, how's your day going?" and their answer is never a positive one. In fact, if you are the teacher who asked how their day was going, you usually regret doing so after listening to their negative answers. They tell you life would be great if they could just have five students removed from their class, if they could have a new principal, if today were Friday, if they were paid more, if they didn't have to write lesson plans, etc. But the fact remains that if five students were removed from their classes, if they did have a new principal, and so on, they would still be negative. And these people are usually even more negative with their students than they are with their coworkers!

Ask an effective teacher how her day is going, and no matter what her current life circumstances, she will always greet you with a smile and say something like, "Great! How's your day going?" This teacher knows the importance of her position as a *teacher* and as a *role model* and, most importantly, as a *professional!* This teacher understands this simple fact: **No matter what your current life circumstances, no matter what you may be dealing with at home, no matter what you may be dealing with at school, and no**

matter how tired you may be, you have to appear happy and enthusiastic—in the name of professionalism and for the sake of the students!

Classroom Solution/Strategy

The strategy is to do what the most effective teachers do—**act professionally no matter what!** Here are a few ways to accomplish that:

♦ Put a smile on your face the moment you drive onto the school campus each morning. Practice keeping it there most of the day.

♦ Offer a kind greeting to everyone you meet.

♦ Remind yourself daily about the importance of modeling appropriate behavior for your students.

♦ Teach everything with enthusiasm.

♦ Resist the urge to speak negatively of anyone.

♦ Resist the urge to complain.

♦ Never tell your coworkers how tired and overworked you are. They are every bit as tired.

♦ Be a problem solver, not a problem seeker.

Bottom Line

Appearing happy and professional is easy when you're having a good day. But is it easy to appear happy and enthusiastic and energetic and professional when you are having a bad day? No, it is not. This is exactly the kind of day, however, when you have to muster all your courage and strength and fake it! If you simply cannot do that, then you should not come to school on that day.

Teaching is tiring work! But **it is much more tiring to be negative all day than it is to be positive!** Your workload will seem overwhelming at times, the meetings will seem endless, the new and innovative methods will keep coming, and, most importantly, the students will continue to need you. These are the challenges we face as teachers, as role models, as those who impact the future. So accept your challenge like a true professional!

47

A Little Guilt Trip Goes a Long Way

A Point to Ponder

When a student is caught misbehaving, he usually feels one of two emotions—guilt or anger. This emotion often stems from the teacher's initial reaction to the misbehavior. If the teacher becomes angry, the student will very likely respond with anger. However, when a student feels guilty instead of angry, his behavior is quite different. A student who feels guilty will very likely improve on the behavior that caused his guilt. Oftentimes, a student who feels angry will very likely defend his actions, regardless of what the actions entailed, and will see to it that the behavior not only continues, but worsens. That's the "I'll show you!" attitude, and it's ineffective.

Helping a student to feel a little *guilty* about his actions can often improve his behavior. Angering a student over his actions almost always causes the behavior to become worse.

Classroom Solution/Strategy

Before we begin speaking of using guilt trips to your advantage in the classroom, we want to state, clearly, that we do not advocate humiliating children. **Putting a student on a bit of a *guilt trip* is quite different from humiliating him.** One helps, the other harms. Having clarified that, let's look into two very different classrooms.

Teacher A is absent from school, and a substitute teacher takes her place. Her *angels* become *demons* on that day. She returns to school to learn of her students' less-than-desirable behavior during her absence. She thinks about it and decides to use *the old guilt trip*. She begins her class by saying, "Don't bother telling me about what happened yesterday. I already know. I know, and I'm heartbroken. I couldn't sleep last night thinking about it, and I probably won't sleep tonight either. I'm just so disappointed. It's hard for me to believe that any of you are even capable of acting the way you did yesterday, and that hurts the most. To think of what that poor substitute teacher had to endure. And to think that you, my wonderful students, were the cause of something so awful! I'm not even able to talk about it anymore now, so let's get started with our lesson." Before she can say anything else, students begin to apologize, some with tears in their eyes. This is because they now feel guilty for what they did.

Do you see what just happened? Their teacher is not mad, but rather she is hurt and disappointed. They didn't push her buttons, but rather they hurt her heart. And because she always treats her students with so much love and respect, they love her and respect her in return. Thus, they are devastated by the thought of disappointing her. They agree, without the prompting of their teacher, to write a letter of apology to the substitute. They assure their teacher that they are sorry, and they truly are! What a wonderful lesson for life!

Teacher B is absent from school, and a substitute teacher takes her place. Her *less-than-angels* become *more-than-demons* on that day. She returns to school to learn of her students' less-than-desirable behavior during her absence. Without giving it any thought at all, she pounces. Her students enter her room, greeted by her glare of anger. Once all are seated, she says, "Well, what do you have to say for yourselves?" No one speaks. No one makes eye contact with her. All eyes are down. She continues with, "Someone had better speak up and explain to me exactly what happened yesterday!" Again, no replies, and no eye contact. She becomes even more enraged, saying, "I know exactly what you did, and every one of you is going to pay a high price for your behavior! How do you think it makes me look when I find out the substitute teacher left school in tears because of you?" She then proceeds to call on particular students, making them stand and humiliating them for their misbehavior. They, of course, say, "It wasn't just me!" The entire class receives several punishments—just random types of punishments as the teacher thinks of new and better ways to make them suffer.

The students are accustomed to this type of reaction from their teacher, as she rarely treats them with respect or dignity. The students are not at all remorseful about the previous day's behavior, because they are too busy feeling humiliated, which spurs feelings of revenge. What a terrible lesson for life!

Bottom Line

 Sometimes, as we as we see in the first scenario, a little guilt trip goes a long way. This strategy, however, should never be over-used. If you use guilt every time a student does something inappropriate, then the student will soon become immune to that strategy and will not take you, his teacher, seriously. Therefore, the entire strategy loses its effectiveness. So **use it, but don't abuse it.**

48

Teach Them to Cope or They'll Create a Way!

A Point to Ponder

 Children cope with stressful situations using the best ways they know. Regrettably, some students don't have many tricks in their bags of coping mechanisms. But the fact is that stressful situations occur in the life of every child, and if we don't teach them how to cope, they'll create their own ways. In a perfect world, all parents would teach their children healthy, appropriate coping mechanisms for dealing with all of life's hardships. We, however, do not live in a perfect world.

Isn't it true that many of your students do not know how to do something as simple as offering an apology? When you ask them to apologize, they trudge forward, fold their arms, and angrily blurt out, "Sorry!" We can all agree that this is not the most endearing, appropriate, or sincere way to offer an apology. How many times do you see a student rolling his eyes, giving a harsh stare, or lashing out in an aggressive manner when he is upset about something? Have you ever stopped to think that these students are actually using the very best or only coping mechanism they know?

As teachers, you all deal with similar situations in your classrooms. Thus, each of you is faced with two choices: **You can choose to do something about it or you can choose to complain about it.** We will assume that you will choose to do something about it, and thus we'll provide you with some strategies for teaching students how to cope with stressful situations.

Classroom Solution/Strategy

There are two main ways that you can teach coping mechanisms to the students in your classroom: teaching and modeling. Although good teaching inherently involves modeling, we treat the two separately here.

By teaching, we mean actually discussing, with your students, acceptable coping mechanisms for dealing with stressful situations and providing them with a variety of ways to deal with such situations appropriately. Don't wait until the stressful situation has already occurred and the student has already acted inappropriately to deal with the problem. Rather, plan specific times to talk about the fact that anger, sadness, frustration, rejection, and the like are all natural human emotions. Then discuss, with your students, some healthy and appropriate ways of dealing with those emotions. Role playing is a very useful strategy in teaching effective coping skills to students. Be particularly careful not to make this a one-shot lesson. Rather, remind students from time to time of appropriate coping strategies, and notice when they actually use these coping strategies.

When we refer to modeling, we mean using your own healthy, appropriate coping mechanisms when dealing with stressful situations. (We refer to this in several places throughout the book when we address the importance of acting professionally at all times and at all costs.) **Remember that students are much more likely to do as you do and not as you say!**

On an ongoing basis, you will need to remind students of appropriate coping mechanisms particular to their situations. And don't ever hesitate to ask for parental support in such situations. If the situation is handled professionally, parents will appreciate your care and concern for their child. We are not suggesting that you call a child's parents every time he does not apologize in an appropriate manner. We are, rather, suggesting that if you realize that a student is struggling in coping with his feelings, and a pattern emerges, it is always a good idea to inform his parents.

Bottom Line

The fact is that all students can benefit from learning effective coping skills. Even those whose parents teach them to cope can still benefit from reminders and practice sessions. Many students do not possess good coping skills, so they develop their own means of coping with emotions, usually to the teacher's surprise and dismay. So nip it in the bud and teach them to cope before the situation arises. Continue to remind them of these skills, model these skills, and praise them when they use the skills.

If their bag of coping skills is hollow
Then model those skills and they will soon follow
They'll handle life's stresses in healthier ways
Which surely will lead to happier days!

49

Listen,
Listen, Listen!

A Point to Ponder

It is often tempting for adults to want to solve children's problems for them, as opposed to enabling them to use their own problem-solving skills. Children don't necessarily need for you to solve their problems for them. Sometimes, they simply need for you to listen to them. Consider the fact that some students have never been *listened to*. They are often told, by adults, "You listen to me!" But, for some children, no one ever really listens to *them*.

With the help of a good listener, children can often solve their own problems. And in order to mature, children *need* to learn to solve some of their own problems. Although it is tempting, we simply cannot jump in and fix everything for them. But we *can* listen! **All effective teachers are good listeners.** And if you ask them how they became good listeners, they will tell you that they continually work hard at being so, constantly reminding themselves that children need good listeners in their lives, every day.

Classroom Solution/Strategy

Being a good listener takes practice. It's a deliberate act that sometimes goes against our grain in that we want so desperately to help others that we sometimes take over and do most of the talking and problem solving instead of simply being quiet and listening.

To be a good listener, you must be aware of what a good listener looks like. Several effective teachers shared some of their **listening strategies** with us so that we might share them with you:

- "I use the term, 'I'm listening' a lot."

- "I interject questions such as 'How did that make you feel when that happened to you?' or 'What do you think you should do?' or 'How do you think you might handle this?' I'm often surprised at how mature their answers are and how adept they are at solving their own problems."

- "I maintain constant eye contact with the student who is speaking."

- "Even though I may not always agree with a student, I always try to let him know that I understand how he must be feeling."

- "I continually tell my students that I am one of the best listeners they will ever meet. Because of this, I hope they will feel free to come to me when they need someone to listen."

- "No matter how busy I am, I always stop what I am doing when a student begins speaking to me. This is to let the student know he has my undivided attention."

- "I nod my head while listening to ensure that the student knows I'm listening."

- "I ask questions while the student is speaking to let him know that I am actually listening to what he is saying and thinking about his current predicament."

- "I lean forward, but not enough to be intrusive. I just want to convey, with my body language, that I am listening."

- "I smile and nod when it's appropriate while listening. And when the situation does not warrant a smile, I am very careful not to appear negative, shocked, disheartened, etc. I want my body language to say that I'm listening and that I care."

- "I often try to paraphrase what the student is telling me in order to let him know I am listening intently and considering what he is saying."

Bottom Line

 We have all experienced the phenomenon of telling a problem to someone who listens intently, only to realize that in sharing the problem we were able to devise our own solution. We often leave that person saying, "Thanks for all of your help." He often replies, "But I didn't do anything." Oh, but he did.

He listened! And sometimes that is exactly what we need—for someone to simply listen to what we have to say. So listen, listen, listen to your students.

> Listen to me when I'm speaking to you
> And please do not say what you think I should do
> Just lend me your ear and it may become clear
> That the answer lies inside of me, not you!

50

Only a Fool Loses His Cool

A Point to Ponder

Pushing My Buttons

I pushed the little button, to summon the elevator
Since I was in a hurry, I needed it sooner, not later

I waited and waited and waited for the elevator to arrive
I pushed the button once then twice—then three times, four times, five
But it never did arrive, you see, and so I took the stairs
A better source of exercise for anyone who dares

And then I got to thinking of the students in my class
Pushing my buttons every day, pushing hard and fast

And there I go reacting, and their "elevator" arrives
They're riding up, they're riding down, and I'm the one with hives

I wonder if I stopped "arriving," if they'd have to take the stairs
I could silence their conniving—the answer to my prayers!

And so I'll start tomorrow, my buttons I will hide
And when they see I won't react, another they'll try to ride

So here's advice to all of you, the teachers who react
Don't let them know your buttons work
They'll stop pushing—that's a fact!

In #17, we discussed the fact that **students should never know that any of their teachers possess pushable buttons, lest the students push those buttons all year long.** The fastest way to identify which teachers reveal their buttons is to listen for the screaming. If you walk into any school and ask students who the *screamers* are, the students always know! All principals can readily name all of their screamers. All teachers know exactly who all of the screamers are on the faculty. And many parents go to extreme measures to ensure that their children are not placed in the classrooms of the screamers.

We do believe that teachers are good people and that most do their very best with what they know. Sadly, no one has ever convinced the screamers that **when you scream at a child in your classroom, you publicly admit that you cannot control your own emotions.** If that is the case, and you cannot control your own emotions, then how can you possibly teach children to control theirs? You cannot.

Questions: Do you do everything your doctor tells you to do? Do you eat exactly the right foods at all times? Do you exercise exactly as much as you should every day? Do you stay away from any and all stressful situations? You don't, do you? Well, just imagine that you go to your doctor for a check-up, he asks you the previous questions, and you answer honestly that you may fall a tad shy in a few of those areas. Your doctor then becomes enraged and begins screaming at you. What will you do? You will very likely leave that office never to return. You will also very likely warn all friends and family members not to return to this very dangerous place! And so you should, because this *professional* has lost his *professionalism*! And that should not be tolerated. So why should it be any different in the classroom? It shouldn't.

As we have discussed throughout the book, **one of our main jobs as teachers is to serve as a good role model for our students, modeling all behaviors we would like them to possess one day.** And none of us want to model for our students that *losing it* when you have had enough is an appropriate response to any situation! On the contrary, we want to model the exact opposite.

Classroom Solution/Strategy

Our strategy here is very simple, yet, for some, we realize it will not be easy. **We challenge you to do what the very best teachers do, to make a promise to your students, on the very first day of school, that though you will always hold them accountable for their actions, you will never raise your voice and scream at them.** Rather, you will always treat them with respect and dignity. Do students hold you to your promises? Yes they do!

By making such a promise, your accomplishment is twofold: (1) You have taken the option of screaming at your students away from yourself, and (2) You have put your students at ease by letting them know that yours is a safe classroom where they will not be threatened. Thus, you have already set the stage for better behavior!

Bottom Line

 Eleanor Roosevelt reminded us that *anger* is one mere letter short of *danger*. She was correct! Don't ever act out of anger with a student. And when you do become angry (because you *are* human), don't ever let your students know that they have made you angry. Disappointed? Yes. Saddened? Yes. Angered? Never!

Only a fool loses his cool. So don't lose your cool, especially at school!

Conclusion

Every student is a special person, worthy and deserving of the very best we have to offer. But offering our best, day in and day out, is not always easy. Teaching effectively takes all we have to give and then some. That's why it is certainly not true that "anyone can be a teacher." Only a very special type of person can truly wear the noble title of *teacher* responsibly, proudly, and deservingly. If you are one of those people, and we believe you are, then don't ever take your tremendous responsibilities lightly. We wish you all the joys and rewards that teaching has to offer, we wish your students all the successes that life has to offer, and we hope we have helped to make you more effective. And one final, important reminder: **There's no such thing as "just a teacher."**

"Just a Teacher"

You don't just hold his hand, you hold his future
You don't just teach her mind, you touch her heart
You don't just wipe a tear, you soothe the soul within
Of all that they become, you are a part

You don't just share a moment, you make a memory
You'll live inside them after you are gone
You'll never know how awesome is your power
Your influence on the world goes on and on

So there's really no such thing as "just a teacher"
You're so much more than words can ever say
You feel it in the moment that you reach her
Or in the way he smiles at you today.

You don't just hold his hand, you hold his future
You don't just teach her mind, you touch her heart
You don't just wipe a tear, you soothe the soul within
Of all that they become, you are a part.

All poetry in this book is the original work of
Annette Breaux.

An Invitation for Your Comments

It has been our pleasure to share with you these 50 ways for improving student behavior. We eagerly invite your input, your suggestions, or any stories you may wish to share for our future writings. Please feel free to contact us at the following e-mail address: author@eyeoneducation.com. Please type our names in the e-mail's subject line.

Annette Breaux
Todd Whitaker

Seven Simple Secrets:
What the BEST Teachers Know and Do!
Annette Breaux and Todd Whitaker

"There is no one I can recommend more highly than Annette Breaux."

Harry K. Wong, author
The First Days of School

This book reveals—

- ◆ The Secret of Classroom Management
- ◆ The Secret of Instruction
- ◆ The Secret of Attitude
- ◆ The Secret of Professionalism
- ◆ The Secret of Effective Discipline
- ◆ The Secret of Motivation and Inspiration

Implementing these secrets will change your life, both in and out of the classroom. But most importantly, implementing these secrets will enhance the lives of every student you teach.

2006, 160 pp. paperback 1-59667-021-5 $29.95 plus shipping and handling

What Great Teachers Do *Differently*:
14 Things That Matter Most
Todd Whitaker

"This book is easy to read and provides essential information. I've ordered copies for every one of my teachers."

Anne Ferrell, Principal
Autrey Hill Middle School
Alpharetta, Georgia

This #1 best selling book has been widely adopted in study groups and professional development programs across the country. It describes the beliefs, behaviors, attitudes, and interactions that form the fabric of life in our best classrooms and schools. It focuses on the specific things that great teachers do…that others do not.

It answers these essential questions—
- Is it high expectations for students that matter?
- How do great teachers respond when students misbehave?
- Do great teachers filter differently than their peers?
- How do the best teachers approach standardized testing?
- How can your teachers gain the same advantages?

2004, 144 pp. paperback 1-930556-69-1 $29.95 plus shipping and handling

101 "Answers" for New Teachers and Their Mentors:
Effective Teaching Tips for Daily Classroom Use
Annette L. Breaux

"There is no one I can recommend more highly than Annette Breaux."

Harry K. Wong, Author of
The First Days of School

This best selling book:

- generates instant impact on teaching and learning
- supports and sustains master classroom teachers who need help mastering their roles as mentors
- stimulates and organizes interactive sessions between new teachers and their mentors
- provides a collection of "thought provokers" and teaching tips for new teachers
- offers common sense strategies for any teacher seeking to be more effective

Topics include:

- Classroom Management
- Discipline
- Relating Lessons to Real Life
- Encouraging Active Student Participation
- Planning
- Professionalism, Attitudes and Behaviors of Effective Teachers

2003 180 pp. paperback 1-930556-48-9 $29.95 plus shipping and handling

Teaching Matters:
Motivating & Inspiring Yourself
Todd and Beth Whitaker

"This book makes you want to be the best teacher you can be."

Nancy Fahnstock
Godby High School
Tallahassee, Florida

Celebrate the teaching life! This book helps teachers:

◆ rekindle the excitement of the first day of school all year long
◆ approach every day in a "Thank God it is Monday" frame of mind
◆ not let negative people ruin your day
◆ fall in love with teaching all over again

Brief Contents

◆ Why You're Worth it
◆ Unexpected Happiness
◆ Could I Have a Refill Please? (Opportunities for Renewal)
◆ Celebrating Yourself
◆ Raise the Praise–Minimize the Criticize
◆ Making School Work for You

2002, 150 pp. paperback 1-930556-35-7 $24.95 plus shipping and handling